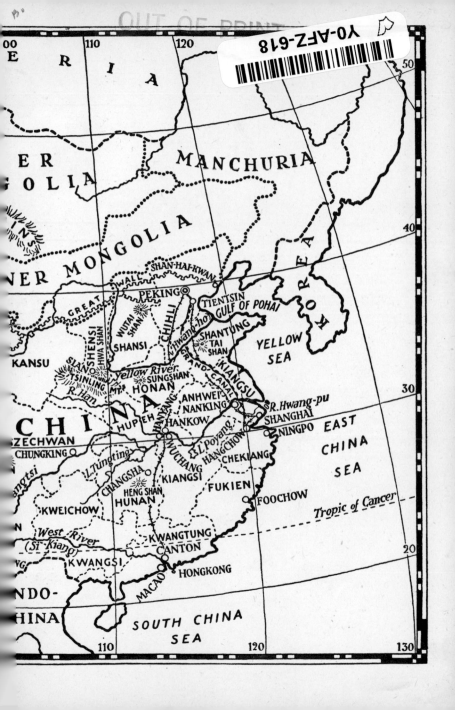

CHINA

HER LIFE AND HER PEOPLE

PAGODA NEAR PEKING

CHINA

HER LIFE AND HER PEOPLE

BY

MILDRED CABLE

AND

FRANCESCA FRENCH

With Maps, Diagrams and Illustrations

UNIVERSITY OF LONDON PRESS Ltd
WARWICK SQUARE, LONDON, E.C.4

FIRST PRINTED . . . . *January*, 1946

AGENTS OVERSEAS

AUSTRALIA AND NEW ZEALAND
W. S. SMART, P.O. Box 120 C.C., SYDNEY, N.S.W.

CANADA: CLARKE, IRWIN & Co., Ltd.
480-486 University Avenue, TORONTO.

INDIA: LONGMANS, GREEN & Co., Ltd.
BOMBAY, CALCUTTA, MADRAS.

SOUTH AFRICA
H. B. TIMMINS, P.O. Box 94, CAPE TOWN.

THIS BOOK IS PRODUCED
IN COMPLETE CONFORMITY WITH THE
AUTHORIZED ECONOMY STANDARDS

Printed in Great Britain for the UNIVERSITY OF LONDON PRESS, LTD.
by HAZELL, WATSON & VINEY, LTD., London and Aylesbury.

PREFACE

THIS book has a purpose. It is written for those who desire a better understanding of China, her country and her people. From the great conflict in which she became involved when she was invaded by Japan, a new China has emerged. Forced into warfare by a cruel enemy who held superiority in every kind of military equipment, she amazed the world by her stability, her confidence and her courage. These qualities form the very character of her people and are the product of long centuries during which, in her isolation, she sought, not to conquer and possess other lands, but rather to cultivate the gifts of peace and quiet. What China discovered and perfected during that period amounted to a great contribution toward world civilization, a contribution which must not be lost. The ferment of the nineteenth and twentieth centuries gradually infected her mood of isolationism, by irresistibly calling on her to take a part in the international business of the world. Commerce invaded her land, western education captured her youth, and Christianity became known to China. Each of these was the applying of a test, and in regard to each China has proved her sterling worth. In commerce she has gained a world-wide reputation for rectitude, in the field of education her young men and women have gained honours in all the lands where they came for advanced study, and as disciples of Christ the Chinese have proved to be true and steadfast, so that to-day there is a strong Chinese Church and among the nation's leaders it is reckoned that about one in six declares himself to be a Christian.

The nations who watch China from afar see her as a wide ocean lashed by the wind to a furious turmoil of riotous waves. At the moment all seems to be disorder and chaos, but the Chinese themselves are aware of a profound stability which is like the untroubled calm of ocean waters which lie too deep for any storm to disturb. Superficial matters are changing in China, but the great foundations of democracy, of reasonableness, of tolerance, of respect for human relationships, of culture and of appreciation of beauty in all its forms remain, and when the storm is passed she will hold a more worthy place among the nations than she has ever yet been accorded. The writers of this book in the course of a lifetime spent in China have watched her emergence and wish to share their knowledge of the Chinese people with all who desire to understand them better, and specially with any expecting to go to the Far East.

The prophet Ezekiel has stated that he sat for seven days where the people sat to whom he came with the Word of the Lord, before he opened his mouth to speak to them. Many national characteristics which are suggested in this volume should be considered by the student before he meets with the Chinese people, and specially before he begins to proclaim the Gospel among them.

ACKNOWLEDGMENTS

FOR permission to use the photographs in this book the authors wish to tender thanks to the following: Exclusive News Agency (E.N.A.), Paul Popper, Dr. Eliot Curwen, Pictorial Press, China Inland Mission (C.I.M.), Topical Press Agency, Ministry of Information (M.O.I.), and The British Museum.

See List of Plates on pages 8, 9 and 10.

CONTENTS

LIST OF PLATES

8

LIST OF PLATES

C—1*

LIST OF PLATES

ILLUSTRATIONS

CHAPTER I

THE MIDDLE KINGDOM

In the days when men still believed the world to be square, the Chinese decided that their own country occupied the very centre of that vast space. Their maps indicated that four great seas surrounded it, and that among them lay various islands inhabited by men whom they called " outer barbarians." It was therefore quite natural that the Chinese should call their own country *Chung-kuo,* which means " Middle Kingdom," and give to all other countries the general name of *Wai-kuo*—" Outside Kingdoms." These names have persisted all through the centuries since long before the Christian era to this very day.

One look at the globe makes it evident that China is a very large country, but no land is important by size alone, and it is the character of her remarkable people which makes her of such great consequence in the world. Including her outlying provinces and dependencies she is nearly seventy-seven times as large as England. Her seaboard is four thousand five hundred miles long, and the seas which form her western and southern boundaries include the South China Sea, the Yellow Sea and the Gulf of Pohai. On the north-west, Sinkiang, China's New Dominion, reaches to the very middle of the Asian continent, and that spot on earth's surface which is the furthest from the seaboard is still within her borders. The northern boundary of Sinkiang touches Siberia, and on the west it is divided from India by the Himalayan Range and the mountains of Tibet. On the south, China is bordered by the lands of Burma and Tonking, being now connected with the former country by the recently constructed Burma Road. China proper is a land of high mountain ranges, of mighty rivers and of vast plains, but her outlying dependencies of Sinkiang and Mongolia contain the widest desert area on the face of the earth.

China is divided into thirty provinces including Tibet, which is a mountainous and sparsely populated country now claiming independence, Mongolia and four Manchurian provinces which have been occupied by the Japanese since 1931. The names of her provinces at first seem puzzling, but when they are understood it is seen that each one has a definite meaning and is a key to the geography of the area which it represents. For example, in the west, which is watered by the great river Yangtse and its three main affluents, the province through which they flow is called " Four Streams " (Szechwan). To the south of Szechwan are high mountain ranges often enveloped in clouds. This has suggested the name of the province beyond, which is " South of the Clouds " (Yunnan). The great Tung-Ting Lake in Central China supplies names for two more provinces, one of which is called " North of the Lake " (Hupeh) and the other " South of the Lake" (Hunan). Further north again mountain ranges serve as boundary between two provinces, called respectively " West of the Hills " (Shansi) and " East of the Hills " (Shantung). Still further north the rushing stream of the Yellow River divides two provinces which are called " North of the River " (Hopeh) and " South of the River " (Honan). On the border of Tibet is " Green Lake " province (Tsinghai), named after the great emerald lake of Kokonor. Bordering the Desert of Gobi is " Summer Tranquillity " (Ninghsia) province, a place where only the summer months are pleasant and where the winter brings terrible blizzards.

China has three main rivers, the two largest of which have their source in the eternal snows of the Tibetan mountains. They divide the country into three wide areas: North China, which is watered by the Yellow River; Central

China by the Yangtse; and South China by the West River. The largest of these rivers is the Yangtse, and in its course of two thousand nine hundred miles it flows west to east through the very centre of China proper, falling 16,000 feet, and finally emptying itself into the East China Sea in an estuary six miles wide, on which the port of Shanghai is situated.

The second in importance is the Hwang-ho, or Yellow River, with a course of two thousand four hundred miles. From its source it flows northward, then turns south, making a huge bend and dividing the provinces of Shensi and Shansi, emptying itself in the Gulf of Pohai in the Yellow Sea. This river is only navigable over limited stretches and at certain times of the year. It takes its name from the colour of its waters. Flowing down through the pale yellow soil of North China, it carries away so much silt that not only is the river itself tinged yellow, but it so discolours the sea into which it flows that this also is called the Yellow Sea.

Twice in the course of the last six hundred years the Yellow River has altered its course over many hundreds of miles, and it is expected to do so again. It constantly deposits so much sediment that the bed is gradually filled up, and in course of time the river rises above the plain and has to be held in by protective banks. The time comes when these inevitably collapse, and the mighty stream spreads over the plain and finds for itself a new outlet to the sea. On account of the havoc caused by flooding the Yellow River has been given the name of " China's Sorrow."

The third most important river of China is the Sikiang or West River. Its length is over one thousand miles, and it rises among the mountains of Yunnan (South of the Clouds). Near its mouth the West River divides and empties itself into the South China Sea through two openings. The

13

northern branch flows through the estuary at the mouth of which is the island and port of Hong Kong, and the southern branch reaches the coast near the port of Macao. Where the West River has room to expand it is fully a mile wide, but at one point it rushes through a gorge which is only 270 yards across. This river plays an important part in the irrigation of China's southern rice-fields.

The highest mountains of China are in the west and in the north. Cutting through Sinkiang from east to west is the line of Heavenly Mountains (Tienshan), the highest peaks of which reach an altitude of 25,000 feet. They form part of the Kunlun Range of Tibet, which extends to the Himalayas. Dividing Tibet from north-west Kansu is the Richthofen Range, named after a renowned German geologist. Here the peaks rise to 20,000 feet and the streams, which all through the summer flow from the eternal snows, create many of the oases in the desert lands of Gobi and Mongolia. The Altai Mountains divide Sinkiang and Mongolia from Russian territory. The word Altai means gold, and the range is so named because of the large amount of that precious metal which is found there. The Mongols of that district wear heavy gold ornaments, and sometimes the buttons of their robes are made of solid gold. The Tsingling Range, which divides North and South China, is a lower continuation of the Kunlun Mountains. Although the hills of Shansi and Shantung do not rise above 6,000 feet, they lend a beautiful ruggedness and great charm to the scenery of North China. On the west the mountain ranges of Tibet also extend southward into the province of Yunnan.

Central China has many lakes, of which two are very important. The Tung-Ting Lake touches the northern border of Hunan (South of the Lake). It is connected with the Yangtse by canals, and during the summer, when water is plentiful, it is filled by the overflow of the river, but during the winter its waters pour back into the Yangtse, thus helping to keep the river at the level necessary for navigation. During the winter the water of the Tung-Ting flows only in the deeper channels, and between them the dry land appears like a series of islands. This lake is 75 miles long and 60 miles broad.

The second largest lake is the Poyang in the coastal province of Kiangsu. It is 90 miles long and 20 miles broad, and is connected with the Grand Canal, for which it also serves as water storage.

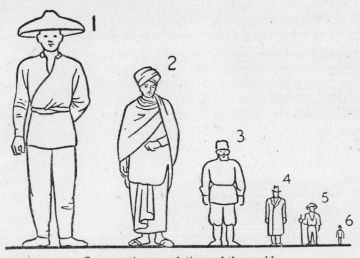

Comparative populations of the world.
1. China.   2. India.   3. Russia.   4. U.S.A.   5. Japan.
6. Great Britain.

In North China the climate is extremely hot in summer and equally cold in winter. The winter is very dry and cloudless, the spring brings sandstorms from the desert areas north and west, and in the later summer there is a rainy season followed by a long fine autumn. In Central China the rainfall is more evenly divided over winter and summer, and in South China the rainfall is much heavier and the damp heat most difficult to endure. The China Sea is subject to typhoons, a terrifying form of whirlwind which causes mountainous seas and is disastrous to shipping. The term "typhoon" is connected with the Chinese words *ta feng*, which mean "the great wind."

If the globe which we study could become a moving picture of the places which it represents, the most startling impression would be one of amazement at the enormous number of people whose home is in the Middle Kingdom and whose mother tongue is Chinese. They are reckoned at four hundred and fifty million, which is about eleven times as many people as there are in England. Moreover, they increase very rapidly, and are such a sturdy race that it is calculated that every fifth child born into the world is Chinese.

It is, however, neither the fact of her size nor of her immense population which gives China a unique place among the nations. Her reliable historic records go back to about 2,000 years B.C., and a great many discoveries of beautiful and useful things are due to the Chinese. She is the oldest living nation with a continuous culture. She has a literature, a philosophy and a wisdom of life entirely her own, and in the realm of art she stands out as the one whose sense of beauty is most highly developed.

CHAPTER II

THE MAKING OF A SEAPORT

THE journey from London to China can be made by several routes. The most usual is to board a steamer in the London Docks, sail through the Bay of Biscay, cross the Mediterranean and pass through the Suez Canal to the Red Sea. The ship goes through the Indian Ocean to the China Sea

SHANGHAI. FOREIGN CONCESSION

SHANGHAI. NATIVE CITY

[Page 16

WILLOW PATTERN TEA HOUSE, SHANGHAI

RICKSHAW PULLERS EAGER FOR A FARE

YANGTSE RAPIDS

IN WIND BOX GORGE, TRACKERS CREEP ON A NARROW LEDGE

Page 17]

and lands its passengers at the port of Shanghai. This sea trip takes about six weeks.

It is also possible to travel by one of the great liners across the Atlantic Ocean, arriving at some port on the east coast of Canada or America. The continent is crossed by train, and another steamer is boarded at one of the West American ports which conveys the passenger to Shanghai over the Pacific Ocean via Japan. Allowing for normal breaks at important places *en route,* five weeks is allowed for this trip.

A more direct journey is to cross the Straits of Dover and take a train through Belgium, Germany and Poland to Moscow. Here the International Trans-Siberian train leaves twice each week for the overland trek across the Ural Mountains, through the Siberian forests, past Lake Baikal and over the plains of Manchuria. About twelve days and nights of unceasing travel will complete the journey to Peking.

As air-routes open up, the quickest and most direct way to China will be via Moscow and across the Desert of Gobi, flying high above the camel caravan track to the towns of Urumchi, Hami and Suchow. The last town is just inside the Great Wall of China on its western side, and from this point an air service connects with Sian, Chungking and Shanghai. The sea journeys are reckoned in weeks, the Trans-Siberian in days, but the air-route in terms of hours.

Shanghai, which is the largest seaport of China, stands at the mouth of the Yangtse. The two syllables Shang-hai mean " On the Sea." It was inevitable that there should be a seaport at the place where this mighty river reaches the sea, yet Shanghai is quite a modern town. Until little over one hundred years ago China had remained so isolated from the world that she felt no need of a port to which foreign vessels could bring their cargoes. When the northern capital Peking had been an important city for nearly two thousand years, Shanghai was still little more than a fishing village where a few groups of fishermen's huts stood on the banks of a small tributary called Huang-pu. In the course of one century a great international seaport has come into being which handles half the export trade of China.

The waters of the Yangtse carry down such a mass of earth and sand to the estuary that big liners are unable to enter the harbour, and all large ships remain at anchor at Wusong, from whence passengers are transferred to the quayside by tender. The bank of silt is called the " Bar," and only smaller cargo vessels can come over it into the harbour.

As the launch steams up the mouth of the river, all aboard are fascinated by the sight of this great eastern port and its strange activities. Everywhere small craft, skilfully plied by Chinese boatmen, skim from ship to ship to pick up refuse thrown out by the crew. Everything which is thrown overboard is immediately salvaged, even though its only use be to serve as manure or fertilizer. Shanghai is reported to be the cleanest port in the East because everything is picked up and put to use. The visitor now receives his first impression of that striking characteristic of the Chinese people—industry and thrift.

All travellers are impressed by the line of buildings which faces the waterside boulevard, or Bund as it is called. Some of them are twenty stories high, and they contain palatial bank buildings, offices of the principal business houses, the largest hotels and the most fashionable clubs. Thus the first sight is that of a modern western town of the most prosperous type. The traffic on the Bund is made up of motor vehicles of every description, but, in and out among them, the swift rickshaw-runners carry their passengers at full speed. There are always groups of well-dressed and prosperous Chinese waiting for friends who are expected by the tender, and rows of splendid cars, drawn up at the landing-stages, wait for the owners or for their friends to disembark.

There is a crowd of agile, eager, excited Chinese, shouting, gesticulating, and all trying to seize the visitor's baggage and thus compel him to make use of their services. These are the luggage-carriers, rickshaw-pullers, money-changers, hotel touts and children begging for cash, and unless the traveller is accompanied by someone accustomed to deal with this rabble he may have a difficult time. At the custom-house he will be questioned by Chinese officials, and asked if he carries any ammunition, any opium, morphia or other deadly drugs. Then, surrounded by his smaller suitcases, he will be whirled off through crowded streets in a rickshaw drawn by a man who keeps up a steady run until he reaches the house to which he has been directed.

Some distance away from the Bund there is a high battlemented wall which surrounds the native city, where four million Chinese live crowded together, mostly in small houses, conducting their lives according to Chinese customs and standards. Outside this city the town is divided into settlements which are controlled by the nationals to which they have been allocated. Shanghai has one International Settlement, and other quarters which are British, American, French, Italian, etc. In another part there was a Japanese settlement where the streets were full of men, women and children wearing Japanese dress, and the shops displayed Japanese signs and sold Japanese goods. It is a strange way of dividing up a town, especially when it is realized that in each concession there is a military guard and a police force made up of the nationals of that particular concession.

In order to understand the system it must be realized that when the British Government went to war with China in 1842 in order to compel her to open up ports for trade and admit opium to the country, the Treaty of Nanking was signed, and the British were given concessions of land on which they might build business houses and residences for themselves. British subjects, moreover, were to be tried according to their own law and by their own consuls. These privileges, which were quickly extended to other nations, constitute what is known as extra-territoriality or, abbreviated, as "extrality." Ever since then in Shanghai and in various other towns of China there have been foreign concessions. This whole system of extrality was revoked in 1942, and the matter of concessions is to be reconsidered as soon as war conditions allow. Until 1842 no European business house might be established in Shanghai, the reason being that the Chinese declared themselves to be self-sufficient, and said that goods from other countries had no interest for them, as their own produce pleased them best in every respect.

As soon as western nations had secured land they went ahead with drainage, building, lighting and town-planning. The result, in the course of one century, is the present seaport with its expanse of quays, its magnificent waterside boulevards, its frontage of international hotels and towering buildings, its cathedrals and its luxurious shopping centres.

In order to lay the foundations for buildings twenty-three stories high, a great deal of engineering work had to be undertaken. The subsoil was merely the mud deposit of an old river-bed, so a base was prepared by first removing the soil to a depth of twenty to thirty feet. Long concrete piles were then driven down, and a concrete raft laid on them to support the towering sky-scrapers. In one of Shanghai's great department stores the foundations were not laid sufficiently firmly, and as a result the whole building sank one foot, so that the flooring of the shop is below street level.

The central street of Shanghai runs north to south and is

named Nanking Road, after the capital of the Chinese Republic. All the roads which run east to west are named after the provinces of China, and those north to south after her largest towns.

The main exports which are shipped from the port are silk, tea, cotton, yarn, pigs' bristles, casings, skins, carpets, wickerwork furniture, and there is also an important industry of silk lingerie and embroidery, some of which is antique and some of which is delicate modern work.

Since 1938 the Japanese army has occupied Shanghai, and for the time being this great port is out of action so far as international trade is concerned. During the war it is only used by Japan as a centre of supply for her armies in China.

CHAPTER III

CHINA'S INLAND PORT

ONE of the busiest quarters of Shanghai is that part which surrounds the riverside wharfs where the large steamers which ply on the Yangtse lade and unlade their passengers and cargoes. Six hundred miles away, upstream, is the inland port of Hankow, and steamers of various navigation companies carry goods up and down the river, on the banks of which are large and populous towns, each of which is a centre of business for local commodities.

At Hankow itself the river is still one mile in width, and it is here that exports from a wide area of inland China are brought. Like Shanghai, Hankow consists of an old native city and modern foreign concessions. Inside the native city the streets are narrow, tortuous and crowded, but along the Bund there is a row of concessions with wide streets and handsome buildings. The word Hankow means " Mouth of the Han," because this is the spot where the great tributary Han flows into the Yangtse.

Hankow is the centre of China's tea trade, and during certain months of the year the streets are fragrant with a delicate perfume of drying tea. The plucked tea-leaves come from the provinces of Hunan, Anhwei, and Kiangsi, and are conditioned and graded by the tea firms of Hankow, the most renowned of which are owned by Russians. Cargoes of cases filled with tea, as we are accustomed to use it in England, are conveyed by river-steamer to Shanghai and then shipped to other countries.

There is, however, another form of tea which is more popular with the people of Central Asia and Mongolia, and this is known as brick-tea. It is prepared by compressing tea-leaves to a solid block, in appearance like a very large dark brown brick, the surface of which is decorated with Chinese, Tibetan or Mongolian script, according to the country for which it is intended. These bricks of tea are conveyed by boat up the inland channels, then by wheelbarrow over steep mountain passes, and finally by cart to Turkestan, by camel to Mongolia, or by yak to Tibet. In the lamaseries of Tibet or the tents of Mongolia a lama or a caravan leader may be seen chipping off a small piece of tea-brick, throwing it into a kettle of boiling water, letting it simmer for some time, and then drinking the pale brown liquid, which is much appreciated as a beverage and has a strange smoky flavour. In those lands where barter is the basis of trade, brick-tea is a valuable commodity, easy to pack and can be handled roughly without deterioration. Its manufacture is a carefully guarded trade secret.

Hankow is also the junction of two main lines of railway. One is the Peking–Hankow line and the other the Canton–Hankow line. So Peking in the far north and Canton in the far south are connected by rail via Hankow.

The waterways which communicate with Hankow bring

huge amounts of raw material to the port. Cotton arrives in large bales which are conveyed by coolies, who carry them on their backs to the firms whose business it is to make merchandise more easy to handle by means of hydraulic pressure. Here a two-hundred pound bale is reduced to a package only two feet by four, in which form it is carried back to the docks and re-shipped to its destination. Large amounts of hemp are handled in Hankow from which rope, string and sacking are made. Sesame seed and goat skins come from Honan, silk, cotton, hides and gypsum from Hupeh, and varnish and wood-oil from the western mountain regions.

On the opposite bank of the Yangtse is the town of Wuchang, and on the other bank of the Han river is a third great city called Hanyang. These three towns form a most important industrial centre. They are connected by ferry, but the bottle-neck outlet of the Han river makes its congested native shipping very difficult to manage. When the north wind blows it will sometimes pile the junks one upon another until they lie in utter confusion, and it is not an uncommon occurrence for people from Hanyang, paying an afternoon call in Hankow, to find themselves held up for several days by the rough waters of the river, which make the use of the ferry impossible. The small craft of the Han and the Yangtse are the sampan, the wupan and the junk. The sampan (three plank width) is the smallest boat on which a family can live, crowded in the tiny cabin. The wupan (five plank width) is a size larger and allows for a second cabin in which a few passengers are housed. These houseboats are propelled either by one man using two oars and facing the direction in which the boat travels, or by means of one rudder-like oar in the stern. The whole family, down to small children, takes a share in management of the boat.

Between Hankow and Shanghai there is little difference

in altitude and the stream flows gently, but above Hankow the current is much more rapid and the upper reaches of the Yangtse flow through gorges which in places narrow the river-bed to a width of barely three hundred yards. The sides of these canyons are sheer walls of rock which rise to a height of four thousand feet. The summits are shaped like the walls of a turret, with rugged peaks and jutting buttresses. The swirling current below forms eddies and rapids which are exceedingly dangerous to navigation. Nevertheless the perseverance of the Chinese people, whose sole living depends upon overcoming the natural obstacles of the river, has succeeded in establishing a waterway, both up-stream and down-stream, over rapids and through gorges, so that the surface of the river carries a constant stream of boats.

Here and there among the gorges are caves several hundred feet up the precipices, and the river-folk make their homes in them. Wherever there is a thin layer of soil over the rock the peasants cultivate it and raise some kind of crop. The difference of water level between the low mid-winter and the summer flood-tide mark is as much as 175 feet.

Since very ancient times river boats have navigated the rapids. They are pulled up-stream by hand-power, but coming down they shoot the rapids at great risk to themselves. Thousands of men are employed as trackers, and their business is a perilous one, hauling the craft by means of ropes made of plaited strips of bamboo. These ropes are so strong that they have been tested to stand the enormous strain of ten thousand pounds to the square inch. In some places the trackers have to walk on narrow footpaths carved in the face of the cliff, and sometimes, at the rapids, they crawl on hands and feet, clawing the cracks of the rock in their effort to bring a loaded junk up-stream. They wear a bandolier which is fastened to the tow-rope with a strong

THE YANGTSE NARROWS AND THE CURRENT IS SWIFT

[Page 24

HANKOW. IN THE OLD CITY THE STREETS ARE NARROW, TORTUOUS
AND CROWDED

THE BUND IS SPACIOUS AND OVERLOOKED BY HANDSOME BUILDINGS

Page 25]

button, for the bamboo ropes are too sharp to be held in the hand. In fastening themselves to the central rope they use a peculiar hitch which can be loosed by a twitch of the wrist, for if caught unawares they might lose their lives if they could not free themselves in a split second.

Wherever possible the peasants plant groves of bamboo, which they use for making all the ropes required for river work. In their own homes also the bamboo serves innumerable purposes. The framework of their huts, the furniture, their rain-capes and hats, cooking utensils, chopsticks, agricultural implements, paper, pens, umbrellas are all made of bamboo, and the young shoots of bamboo supply a most delicious vegetable.

Among the most important towns situated on the banks of the Yangtse are Nanking, which is now the capital of the Chinese Republic, and Chungking, which is the war-time seat of Government and the residence of Generalissimo Chiang Kai Shek and Madame Chiang.

CHAPTER IV

A UNIQUE WALL, CANAL AND ROAD

WHEN China plans a wall, digs a canal or makes a new road she does it on such a grand scale that it becomes something which the whole world talks about. The Great Wall, the Grand Canal, and the Burma Road have each in turn been described as one of the wonders of the world. Each was built with a definite national aim, and each has served the purpose for which it was intended.

The Great Wall of China was in process of being built two thousand two hundred years ago, but it is still an imposing structure which people travel long distances to see.

It begins at Shan-hai-kwan, north of Peking, and can be followed in a westerly direction for about 1,500 miles. Like some great serpent it stretches over mountain ranges, across deep ravines and valleys, and at one point it divides into two branches, forming a great loop which encircles the city of Kalgan. Further north-west it divides the provinces of Shansi, Shensi and Kansu from Mongolia, and finally it seals China's outlet to the Gobi Desert with a battlemented fortress called Kia-yu-kwan (Barrier of the Pleasant Valley). At its east end, which is on the seaboard, the height of the wall is twenty to thirty feet and its base is fifteen to twenty-five feet thick. The summit is paved, and presents a level surface like a promenade which is twelve feet wide. The greater portion of the wall is made of earth, strengthened as required with a facing of round boulders, but in the valley bottoms and on mountain passes it is supported by masonry and brickwork. About every two hundred yards a squat tower forty feet high was erected to shelter soldiers and supply an outlook over the Mongolian plain, which was enemy land. At its highest point the wall stands four thousand feet above sea level. The portion which is most frequently visited is built among the bare hills beyond Peking, and there it is in such good repair that in the course of the present war it has again served as a military road for the transit of troops on the march. In ancient days the fact that it ensured a reliable marching road for the army was one of its chief advantages.

Further west the wall was less strongly built, and much of it is now in very bad condition, but at Kia-yu-kwan the fort is worthy of its name, for its walls within walls and inner and outer gates make of it an imposing military outpost. Outside the outermost gate, and within sight of the Gobi, a tall stone tablet is erected on which are inscribed Chinese ideographs meaning " Earth's Greatest Barrier."

For many centuries before the Christian era China's most troublesome enemies were the nomad hordes who were tent-dwellers of the bleak Mongolian plain. These hardy people formed bands of roving horsemen, constantly raiding their more civilized and peaceable neighbours, the Chinese. They attacked peaceful farming centres, they looted towns and villages, and galloped back to their encampments carrying off booty and prisoners. From time to time these raids developed into extensive campaigns. The Chinese, with their superior military strategy, were a match for the Huns, except that the latter came and went so rapidly on their sturdy steppe-land ponies that they outwitted the Chinese army. In order to stop these raids the Chinese built this Great Wall of such a height that no horseman could get over it without leaving his mount behind, and deprived of their horses the Huns were no match for the nimble Chinese.

Warfare with the barbarian nomads brought about the building of the Great Wall, and it was fear that in the event of maritime war there might be shortage of food in Peking that made the Chinese plan that other great undertaking known as the Grand Canal. The southern and central provinces are the " rice-bowl " of China because of the swampy nature of their land, in which rice grows so prolifically. In normal times fleets of junks carried this rice through the China Sea to the populous and rich northern towns, but in time of war the enemy attacked the junks and Peking starved. A plan was therefore devised of digging a canal which, even in wartime, could serve for the transport of food.

This great canal was commenced in 486 B.C., and ever since that time has remained a valuable, busy and magnificent water thoroughfare with a total length of twelve hundred miles, stretching from Hangchow in the south to Tientsin in the north. Under Imperial Government the provincial taxes were paid in kind and were handed over in Peking; therefore innumerable junks were required to transport the tax-grain down the Yangtse and along the Grand Canal to the Imperial City.

The canal borders are populous with many large towns and innumerable villages, and the boat life which it sustains is full of interest. The sampan, the wupan, the junk and steam-launches are all found on its waters, and a large population of water-folk has no home except the cabin of a house-boat.

The canal varies considerably in width according to locality. In its handsomest though not widest reaches it is spanned by elegant stone bridges, and where it meets the Yangtse it extends to make room for a great influx of shipping. Further north it touches the waters of the Poyang Lake, but over long stretches the bed of the canal has been raised by the deposit of silt which is washed into it. Consequently in course of time the banks have been lifted until now the canal stands high above the surrounding land. This constitutes a great danger, for at times of unusual spate, in spite of strenuous efforts to keep the dykes intact, they are liable to reach breaking point at one place or another, and disastrous floods occur in which human beings are drowned and cultivated land is submerged, causing widespread famine. With all their many ingenious devices, the Chinese never discovered the secret of building locks, and where the varying levels of the canal make navigation difficult they construct a barrage, over which empty boats are hauled by windlasses worked by man-power. The delays caused by this inevitably slow system are considerable, and make travel by river boat on the Grand Canal a very leisured performance.

The third construction of China which has been classed as one of the wonders of the world is the Burma Road, and it was again through facing the emergencies of war that it came into being. China was always shut in on her southern side, and debarred from overland communication with her neighbours by the mountainous nature of the land. There existed a very ancient caravan trail leading to Burma, but the rough country made it unusable by any save pack-animal traffic. Of recent years the aggression of Japan made the building of a Burma motor road imperative, and after the most careful survey it was decided that the best line for the new road lay over the track of the old one. The road was begun in 1937. It is seven hundred and seventy-two miles long, commencing at the town of Kunming in the province of Yunnan and ending at Lashio in Burma. It crosses two very large rivers, the Mekong and the Salween, the former of which flows between mountains eight thousand feet high, while the width of the Salween is as much as eight hundred feet. The bridges of the old caravan route were made of rope, and were no wider than four feet over a span of three hundred feet. The crossing of these bridges, even on foot, was a perilous business. In the swampy land at river level summer heat is intense, and malaria-carrying mosquitoes are so numerous that there was terrible mortality among the bands of labourers who built this portion of the road.

The road rises to a maximum height of four thousand feet in twenty miles. Such gradients necessitate a series of terrifying hairpin bends on roads only eight feet wide which are skirted by a two-thousand foot precipice. The danger in driving is such that in the year 1940 statistics showed that two lorries and three lives were daily sacrificed through the driver losing control and the car plunging over the embankment. The work of levelling gradients and widening tracks is always being carried on, so that, gradually, risk to life will be lessened.

The area through which the Burma Road passes has been described as " the most heart-breaking country in the world," for, added to such difficulties as those already mentioned, there is a rainy season lasting from June to October when torrential rains invariably cause landslips which temporarily obliterate the motor road. The Chinese people made this road with the same patience and indomitable perseverance as they showed in constructing the Great Wall and the Grand Canal. It was done by the combined effort of men, women and children, using often the most primitive tools such as long hoes and stone-rollers; in fact, much of the debris was removed in baskets by the women and children. At one spot there is an inscription in Chinese painted on the edge of a precipitous cutting in the cliff. It reads thus: " This road was built by the natives of this district, without the aid of foreign implements."

Very few actions on the part of foreign nations have angered the Chinese people more than the closing of the Burma Road by the British Government in 1940. At the end of 1939 the Indo-Chinese railway and the Burma Road were carrying more than three-quarters of Free China's imports, and psychologically the blow was a cruel one. British statesmen considered this to be a necessary action in order to secure sufficient respite after the fall of France to enable Britain to temporize with Japan, but China felt herself deserted by one of her best friends, and it is easy to understand her intense feeling of anger and distress, with her ports in enemy hands, much of her land occupied by enemy forces, and now her only means of supply cut off. When British public opinion was aroused the Burma Road was re-opened, and even those in high places expressed deep regret that the step had ever been considered necessary.

China values her western outlet so much that a new highway is in process of construction which will connect West China with India via Assam. China's Emperor once told a British monarch that he needed no supplies from the rest of the world, as China was entirely self-sufficient. It is tragic that this peace-loving nation is compelled to depend on Westerners for weapons of death made necessary not by her own aggressiveness but by the cruelty of an enemy who seized her land and murdered her people.

CHAPTER V

THE NORTHERN CAPITAL

IN the course of her long history China has had many successive capital cities, but the most renowned of them is Peking, where the Manchu Emperor set up his throne in 1644. After the establishment of the Chinese Republic in 1912 the seat of government moved to Nanking (Southern Capital), and Peking (Northern Capital) changed its name to Peiping (Northern Plain). Twelve centuries before Christ there was already a town on this site, and although destroyed many times it was always reconstructed.

The Imperial City was built on the same plan as every Chinese *Yamen* or official residence. In the old Chinese *Yamen* every visitor passed through a series of courtyards leading from one to another until he reached the innermost court, where the Mandarin had his private apartments. To walk uninvited to that court was an offence punishable by death. Peking is designed on the same pattern, but on such a grandiose scale that different quarters of the whole huge city stand for the courtyards of the *Yamen*. The Emperor lived at its very centre in the Imperial Palace, which was a place of utter seclusion and always called the Forbidden City.

The outer walls of Peking form a vast rectangle ten miles in length and six miles in width, and the city which they nclose is divided by a few wide streets, between which are labyrinths of narrow alleys. In the Tatar city are the residential quarters of the inhabitants, and, though to the stranger they appear crowded, yet it would be impossible to overstate the beauty of the houses which often lie behind such an unassuming frontage. Each has a landscape garden with moon door, small lotus ponds and weeping willows. Though not large, such a garden is designed with a perfect sense of fitness and proportion. The houses are usually one-storied, built round a courtyard, and are admirably designed. The furnishings and decoration of the rooms are in perfect keeping with the surroundings. The Imperial Court and the wealthy population of Peking so cultivated appreciation of beauty in form, colour and material that the architecture, the gardens, the decoration and the furnishing of their palaces and homes reached perfection point.

In the south-east corner of Peking is the Observatory, in which some old astronomical instruments are preserved. The bronze Armillary Sphere and the Astrolabe were made about 1272 by Persian astronomers whom Kublai Khan brought to China in his train. They have been exposed to the weather in the open courtyard of the Observatory for more than six hundred years, but are still the finest known specimens of bronze in the world.

The Imperial City contains the Universities, many temples and various public buildings. At its centre is the Purple Forbidden City, as its full title stands, surrounded by a wide moat full of lotus plants. The surface of the water is covered by their circular leaves, and in the flowering season lovely white and pink blossoms stand erect and magnificent above them. In Imperial days the name Forbidden City meant all that the words imply, and the punishment inflicted for passing through its gates without proper authority was one hundred blows of the bamboo.

Inside were a succession of spacious throne-halls and palaces, which were the living quarters of the Emperor and such members of the Imperial family as had a right to live

TRACKERS TOWING JUNKS WITH BAMBOO ROPES

THE GRAND CANAL AT TIENTSIN

[Page 32

CHINA'S GREAT WALL

ANCESTRAL HALL.   TEMPLE OF HEAVEN, PEKING

there. The Pavilions of Learning, which contained the Imperial Library, the administration buildings of the Imperial household and almost innumerable palaces and halls, each of which was dedicated to some particular use, stood in the vast spaces which surrounded the living quarters. Each building had a high-sounding title, such as " The Hall of Supreme Harmony " for a throne-room, " The Palace of Established Happiness," where royal portraits were preserved, " The Hall of Industrious Energy," which was one of the Imperial schoolrooms. "The Hall for Blending Creative Forces " held the marriage certificates of the Empresses written on plaques of gold, and behind the palaces of " Cloudless Heaven " and " Tranquil Earth " was the garden exclusively reserved for members of the Imperial family. It was a place of great charm and beauty, with grottoes and winding pathways among groves of " thousand-year cedars."

There was one Hall, however, quite unlike that in any other palace. Lofty, large and unfurnished, the floor space was covered with rocks built up to represent a rugged mountain with a narrow path leading from one rock cave to another. Among the rocks of this mountain the Emperor came from time to time to meditate on the quest of hermits and others who chose a life of poverty that they might the better understand deeper things. In fact this strange building was a " thinking room."

With the proclamation of Republican Government for China, the full glory of the Forbidden City departed, and to-day the halls, temples and living apartments are open to the public, while the former Emperor lives under Japanese control in Manchuria. Until occupation by the Japanese the palaces still held a unique collection of ,bronzes, jade carvings, lacquered boxes, enamels, ivories, exquisite blackwood furniture, and a hall full of jewel-plants, each one of which was deftly made of jade, cornelian, malachite and all manner of lovely coloured stones.

Outside the Inner Wall of Peking are the vast parks which hold the Hall of Agriculture and the Temple of Heaven. These were visited on certain festivals by the Emperor himself. At springtime, when the earth is disturbed from her long winter sleep, the Emperor went to the Hall of Agriculture, and there he ploughed a furrow and threw a handful of the five kinds of grain on to the land. These grains were symbolic of the produce by which man lives—rice, wheat, millet, hemp and pulse. Thus the Emperor himself acknowledged his dependence on the bounty of heaven and, by the action of ploughing, did honour to all who till the soil.

The general title which belonged to all rulers of China was " Son of Heaven." Once a year, on the longest night of the winter, December 21, after severe fasting, the " Son of Heaven " went to the enclosure which surrounds the Temple of Heaven. The principal altar of the Temple is a triple circular terrace of white marble. It rises tier above tier, and the summit is reached by a wide stairway. The platform is paved in nine concentric circles with a circular stone as centre. The Emperor, standing on this centre stone, surrounded by the nine concentric circles beyond which was the vast boundary of the horizon, was thought of by his people as standing at the centre of the universe. At midnight, leaving the pavilion where he had put aside his regal robes and clothed himself in the simplest dress, the Son of Heaven walked alone and unattended to the high platform, and there knelt in the double capacity of ruler and priest, offering the homage of his people to the great *Tien* who, to the Chinese, is Lord of Heaven and Earth. While he prayed a white bull was slain and burnt as sacrifice at the foot of the altar. The Chinese have a proverb which says, " Only through knowledge of the past can the present be understood," and truly it is only through knowledge of China's background that the greatness of her people can be appreciated.

Outside Peking, and about seven miles to the east of the Great Wall, is a quiet valley which holds the tombs of thirteen emperors of the Ming dynasty. The spacious burial ground is so stately and so dignified that it is acknowledged to be one of the finest architectural schemes in the world. The tombs are not laid in chronological order, but are distributed over the valley according as each sovereign chose for himself a site suited to the demands of his horoscope. The Triumphal Way opens with a five-arched gateway which stands in the open country, and beyond it spreads the valley of dead emperors and an avenue which is called "The Spirit Road for the Mausolea." The greatest sculptors of the Ming period shaped the stone figures which seem to guard the avenue, leading to the distant temples and to the sepulchres. The Triumphal Way is two-thirds of a mile long, and is lined with eighteen pairs of colossal statues of men and animals. There are sitting and standing lions, kneeling and standing camels, four elephants, four horses and unicorns, with figures of stately warriors in grey stone and officials in full civil dress or clad in armour and wearing fantastic helmets.

Where the road passes through the triple "Dragon and Phœnix Gate" most of the thirteen scattered tombs can be seen. The most beautiful of them holds the body of Yung Loh (1402-1424). The sepulchre is reached through an outer courtyard in which are ancient and twisted trees, then an inner court on which opens the Sacrificial Hall where the rites of ancestral worship have been performed in Yung Loh's honour by the long line of emperors who succeeded him. This Hall is the largest building in China, and measures seventy yards by thirty yards. The roof is supported by forty pillars shaped from tree-trunks each more than a yard in diameter and sixty feet high. It is an empty temple save for a simple wooden table for offerings, and a stand for the tablet on which the dead man's name is inscribed and in which his spirit is supposed to rest.

The tomb itself lies beyond a further courtyard which is behind the temple and through a vaulted passage forty yards long which conceals a stone stairway rising to the grave-chamber where the coffin was laid. The entrance to the vaulted passage is closed by a special device, for inside and behind the door a round hole was cut in the stone flooring and a large ball of stone so placed that when the door was shut it fell into the hole and prevented the door from ever being opened again.

CHAPTER VI

READING, WRITING AND RECKONING

LEARNING to read and to write takes a very large part in the life of a Chinese boy or girl. The Chinese language has no alphabet; every word is a monosyllable such as ma, li, chu, fan, wang, and each word is represented by an ideograph or picture. Some of the ideographs are very simple and made up of only two or three strokes, while another may be so elaborate as to require twenty-seven strokes of the pen to form it, yet it is still a monosyllable.

Some of the earliest writing goes back as far as eighteen hundred years before Christ, and at that time the ideographs showed a strong likeness to the object they represented. The sign for rain was like drops falling from the sky; that for cow was shaped like the horns of cattle; and the one for moon was crescent-shaped. With the progress of thought the number of ideographs increased enormously through the centuries. For example, the sign for mouth is a square opening 🜲 (pronounced co), but when something solid proceeds from it it becomes tongue 舌 (pronounced share), and when breath is represented as coming from the mouth the ideograph is the word for speech 言 (pronounced yen).

A combination of characters may represent a whole series of words all pronounced the same, but each with a different meaning. For example, *bao* means a packet; *bao* and a hand means to carry; *bao* and a foot means to run; *bao* and water is a bubble; *bao* and rain means hail, and many other combinations could be mentioned. At the

A drawing to scale to illustrate the world's most widely spoken languages.

present time new combinations are always being formed in order to represent new ideas. A Chinese schoolboy has to be familiar with about two thousand ideographs before he can read ordinary books, and advanced education demands the free use of at least ten thousand characters.

To the westerner the chief difficulty of the Chinese language is the fact that it is tonal, and that by means of various inflections a totally different meaning is given to one word; for example, *fan* in a high tone means food, but *fan* in a low tone means tumult. It sounds very complicated to a westerner, but no Chinese thinks of tones as difficult, nor does he ever make a mistake in using them. He learns the tone or inflection with the word, and quite unconsciously uses all five tones correctly. Every language has its own subtle rhythms which are unnoticed by the people of the land, but become evident when a foreigner speaks. It is by the correct use of these rhythms that a stranger makes himself easily understood.

If the reading of Chinese is difficult its writing is far more so, and is only acquired by the exercise of much patience and concentration. It is spoken of as the art of Chinese calligraphy, and the man or woman who can use the brush well and write the characters with distinction is considered an artist of no mean order. At school each child is provided with articles which are called " the four treasures of the room of literature "—a brush, a brush-stand, a block of ink and a stone inkslab. The ink is made from the soot of burnt pinewood or lampblack, mixed with oil, allowed to solidify and moulded into flat or round sticks decorated with designs in gilt characters. The stick is ground on the inkslab with a little water until the fluid is neither too thick nor too thin. While rubbing down the ink the child is taught to make its mind calm and quiet, so that the sacred characters are not used carelessly or unworthily. The writing-brush is stroked on the inkslab until the hair is brought to a fine point. This brush is made of animal hair tied together and fixed into a hollow reed or thin bamboo stem. For small writing and delicate characters rabbit's hair is the most popular, but for large characters sheep's hair is best. In earliest times, before the brush was invented, writing was done by dipping a piece of frayed bamboo into ink and using it as a pencil. The brush as now used was invented in the third century B.C.

Since the time of the Revolution (1911) China's leaders have been deeply concerned about the widespread illiteracy of the people. At that time only twenty out of every hundred could read and write. In order to bring literacy within reach of the masses every effort has been made to simplify the complicated system of reading and writing, and two methods have been used, both of which have been amazingly successful. A phonetic script was compiled which has been widely used in Government and Missionary schools. The sounds are represented by forty signs used singly or in combination. For example, the complicated 霍 is written phonetically 尾 , yet both represent the sound " ho." It was found that by means of this system complete illiterates could be taught to read in a remarkably short time. The Government school-books soon introduced the plan of printing the shorthand phonetic by the side of each new ideograph, and this has been of immense help to students.

The other way of helping illiterates is based on a system of limiting the written language to twelve hundred words, and a whole series of books has been compiled which use only these twelve hundred characters. Since 1926 ten million people have learnt this system of reading at a cost to the Government of only $1.40 (at par 2s. 6d.) per pupil. The teaching has been largely undertaken by young Chinese patriots, who responded enthusiastically to the slogan " The illiterate is a blind man. Can you stand to see three-quarters of China blind?" Village schools, open-air classes and holiday groups have been organized by students who were determined to make the people literate. In one province a law was passed that every illiterate would be taxed until he had learned the twelve hundred characters and passed an examination on them. The organizer of this scheme was James Yen, a young Chinese who had studied in an American University, and is popularly known as Jimmy Yen.

Christian missionary work has always been in the van-guard of the literacy campaign, and many of the best teachers have been gathered from men and women who were trained in Mission schools. It has been the aim of all Christian Missions that the converts should be able to read, and all who were willing have been thoroughly taught so that they can read the Bible for themselves. At the beginning of this century very few women and girls could read, but Mission schools were pioneers in the education of girls in the days when it required great courage to come to school and learn to read like their brothers. Now there are elementary girls' government schools everywhere, and they can continue their education in High School, College and University.

Although western systems of arithmetic and mathematics are now taught in all schools, the Chinese method of reckoning is still by the use of a calculating tray called an *abacus*. It is a wooden frame on which a number of beads are strung on parallel lines, and it is based upon the decimal system. In the largest banks Chinese clerks and cashiers use the *abacus,* and with its help they reckon up long accounts with amazing rapidity and accuracy. Illiterate peasants accustom themselves to mental calculation, and when buying and selling will reckon any account without the use of pencil or *abacus* so accurately that no one can cheat them. In all large transactions Chinese merchants do not discuss prices aloud. The buyer and the seller each put a hand up the other man's sleeve and by movements of the fingers indicate the price asked and accepted. The bargaining goes on in silence until the transaction is complete.

ASTRONOMICAL INSTRUMENTS AT PEKING OBSERVATORY, CON-
STRUCTED BY PERSIAN ASTRONOMERS

PEKING SHOPS

CHAPTER VII

THE HUNDRED NAMES PEOPLE

ONE of the strangest school-books that the Chinese boy handles when he first goes to school is called " The Book of a Hundred Names." It is, in fact, a list of all the surnames found in the country: Wang, Li, Ma, Feng, Chiang and many others, but there are no fancy names with strange pronunciations, nor is any name reckoned to be more honourable than another, and the name of every Chinese is included in the book. The name given to a European on his Chinese passport is the one selected from this same volume which has the nearest sound to his own family name. This very democratic " Who's Who " is memorized by innumerable Chinese boys and girls, and every child must learn to write it. It represents what the Chinese call " the people of the hundred names "—and a grand people they are, for they live well-ordered, industrious lives, content with what the day may bring, and always seek to fulfil their responsibilities towards the clan to which they belong.

In the Chinese home everything is done according to established custom. In the house of any one of the " Hundred Names People," for example, there is a definite place for the parents' living-room, for that of the elder son, the second and third son, etc., etc. Inside the rooms there is an ordered arrangement for the tables and for each chair, and every visitor knows at once on which chair he should sit and where his host will stand to receive him.

The " people of the hundred names " are lovers of peace and quiet. The vast majority (87 per cent.) live in villages, cultivating their land industriously, and each clan is self-sufficient. The wheat or rice which is the staple diet is grown on the family land, vegetables are produced as required, and sufficient cotton is grown so that the whole family may have garments to wear. The women pick the cotton, spin and weave it, then dye it with the indigo plant from their own fields. They cut up the lengths of cloth as needed, and make the simple but adequate and comfortable Chinese coats and trousers which are worn both by men and women. In wintertime these garments are made double and wadded with home-grown cotton-wool, or, in North China, with hair from the family camels. Even the shoes are home-made. Every scrap of worn material is saved to serve as filling for the soles, which are a quarter of an inch thick, and these are stitched through with home-made string of hemp fibre. The uppers are made of strong hand-woven cotton carefully cut to measure, and the shoes are so well and strongly stitched that even schoolboys can wear them for a long time, and farmers do all their heaviest work in shoes made for them by their wives.

One son in a family may hold an official position, another may be a teacher, another organize and control the great caravan of camels which he takes to Peking each year laden with cotton, pelts or tobacco, bringing back foreign goods such as enamelware and fancy articles for sale in the markets near his own farm. Another son may be a business magnate who travels abroad and controls large interests, while other men of the family will do the farming, and one may work in a coal-mine or have a small shop or tea-house in a neighbouring village—it is quite immaterial what each man's occupation may be—the clan, the family, that is the centre of life for them all, and none will despise the other because his vocation or trade seems more humble or brings in less money. The contribution of each is recognized as being essential to communal life.

When a son marries, it has been the custom to bring his bride to the family home, where she should wait upon her mother-in-law and take her place in the wide circle of the clan. In modern China this is rapidly changing, and the young people do not now necessarily live with their parents. The fact, however, remains that the family tradition is such that each generation feels itself to be part of a great chain which links the past with the future. The ancestors are worshipped and their spirits are said to be present in the place where their names are recorded. Every household shrine holds wooden tablets inscribed with the names of the dead, and every clan has an ancestral temple where incense is burnt and where there are ceremonial offerings of food. On all occasions when family life is affected, as by a marriage or a death, formal announcements are made to the ancestors as though they were still present. Wherever the Chinese may be, home has a tremendous attraction for them, and they always desire to be buried among those mounds of earth surrounded with trees where the bodies of their forefathers are laid.

The clan is accustomed to express its unity in the recurring festivals which draw its members together. Apart from special occasions such as rejoicings at births, merriment at marriages and long rituals at funerals, there are seasonal festivities throughout the year, which is divided into exact periods, beginning with New Year's Day. The Chinese have always observed the lunar calendar, and New Year's Day generally fell toward the beginning of February. This first day of the first moon was China's greatest day of the year, but when the Republican Government decreed that January the first was now the date on which the year began, the people said: " Who can rejoice in the midst of mid-winter cold? Moreover, this change of calendar must necessarily offend the spirits that guard and control our lives." Orders were posted in all the towns and gongs were beaten on the streets to call public attention to the fact that January 1st was New Year's Day, and that omission to keep it as such would result in a heavy fine. On the appointed day fresh scarlet scrolls were obediently posted outside the doors, official calls were duly paid and the shops were kept shut, but not until six weeks later, on the first day of the first moon, did the " Hundred Names People " give themselves up to feasting, gaiety and merry-making. Thus public opinion actually carried the day. Gradually, however, such pressure has been brought to bear on the populace that the old customs are vanishing in many of the large towns, but in all the country places the first day of the first moon is still the people's holiday.

On the 15th of the first moon the New Year holiday came to an end with the Feast of Lanterns, when every variety of lantern was carried in procession. Some were in the shape of fifteen-foot-long dragons and other magnificent contrivances, while others were delicately made in the form of flowers, birds and insects. On the day known as " Clear Brightness," which falls in early spring, the family graves are always repaired. In early summer comes the period of " Sprouting Corn," followed by " Excited Insects," " Small Heat " and " Great Heat," then " Beginning of Autumn," " Small Cold " and " Great Cold." Seasonable weather can be depended upon, and no one thinks of undertaking a long journey, unless compelled to do so, during the days of " Great Heat " or " Great Cold."

There is one festival which is now known all over the world, and is spoken of as " China's Double Tenth " — that is, the tenth day of the tenth month (October 10th), the day on which the establishment of the Chinese Republic is celebrated. On that occasion London joins with her Ally in demonstrations and rejoicing. Gradually, with changing conditions, many of the old festivals will be less rigidly observed, but they are so interwoven with the fabric of

China's thought that it will be many generations before the Hundred Names People allow them to fall into complete oblivion.

CHAPTER VIII

THE RICHES OF THE LAND

CHINA is perhaps unique among the countries of the world in that she is able to supply all the necessities of a civilized life to her own people. Through many long centuries the western nations were eager to do business with China, but this was never encouraged by the Chinese themselves. They needed neither the European nor his goods, and there is a famous letter from Chien Lung, Emperor of China (1736-1796), which was written to King George III and sent back with Lord Macartney's Mission in 1793. It reads:

" You, O King, live in a distant region, but desiring humbly to share the blessings of our civilization, you have sent an embassy respectfully bearing your letter.

" Our dynasty's majestic virtue has reached every country under heaven, and kings of all nations have sent their tribute by land and sea. We possess all things; we are not interested in strange and costly objects, and we have no use for your country's products. I have accepted your tribute offerings only because of your devotion which made you send them so far.

" Your letter shows a respectful humility, and I have entertained your ambassador, have given him many gifts, and am sending ·you, O King, valuable presents of which I enclose a list. Receive them reverently.

" As to your request to send an ambassador to live at my Heavenly Court, this request cannot˙ possibly be

45

granted. Any European living in Peking is forbidden to leave China or to write to his own country, so you would gain nothing by having an ambassador here. Besides, there are many other nations in Europe beside your own; if all of them asked to come to our Court, how could we possibly consent? Can our dynasty change all its ways and habits in order to do what you ask?

" Your ambassador asks us to allow your ships to trade at other ports beside Canton. This request is refused. Trade may be carried on only at Canton.

" The request that your merchants may store and trade their goods in Peking is also impracticable. My Capital is the hub and centre around which all the quarters of the earth revolve. Its laws are very strict and no foreigner has ever been allowed to trade there. This request is also refused.

" Your ambassador has asked permission to have your religion taught in China. Since the beginning of history, wise emperors and sages have given China a religion which has been followed by the millions of my subjects. We do not need any foreign teaching. The request is utterly unreasonable.

" I have always shown the greatest kindness to tribute embassies from kingdoms which truly long for the blessings of civilization, but your demands are contrary to the customs of our dynasty and would bring no good result. It is your duty to understand my feelings and reverently to obey my instructions."

Lord Macartney carried this sealed letter home thinking that his mission had been successful, for he had been greatly impressed by the reception accorded him. What the Emperor said was true: China had all she needed because of the ceaseless industry of her people, who, in spite of a rapidly increasing population, maintained supplies sufficient for her own necessities.

The principal product of the southern provinces is rice, which is the staple food of the majority of Chinese. The word " rice " has become interchangeable with the word " food," so that the idiom for the common greeting, " Have you taken food?" is " Have you eaten rice?" and " What is your meal time?" becomes " At what o'clock do you eat rice?" This grain is cultivated in three main varieties: (1) Ordinary rice (Oryza sativa), which must be planted out in land kept under water and which has been ploughed by the water buffalo. Between the rice plantations is a raised path on which people can walk dry-shod, but all the cultivation is done in the submerged part of the field.

(2) Mountain rice (Oryza montana) grows on land which is not under water but which is watered by abundant rains.

(3) Glutinous rice (Oryza glutinosa) is mainly used for the distilling of spirit and for making rice-cakes.

Rice is generally grown in special seed-raising beds, and the seedlings are transplanted by hand into submerged fields where, as the plants grow, the water can be gradually drained off to a lower level. Although water is essential to the root and lower part of the plant, it must never be completely under water, and when the grain is full in the ear only a small amount of moisture is needed. The rice is stored in the condition where it is called " paddy," that is to say, before it has been freed from the husk. The main rice-producing areas are in the delta land around Canton and among the valleys of the Yangtse and its tributaries.

Another important product of the south is tea (Camellia thea). The infusion which we call tea is first mentioned in Chinese annals in the year A.D. 500, but the English people only began to drink tea in the middle of the seventeenth century, and then it cost six to ten pounds per lb. Tea grows well even in rather poor soil, but only thrives where it receives moisture both during the winter and the summer. The town of Hankow is the main centre of the tea trade, and the harvested leaves are conveyed there by boat. The demand for China tea has so much increased during recent years that the crop is never sufficient to meet the needs of the market.

Sugar cane is grown in large quantities, but particularly on the hot plains around Hong Kong.

Silk is one of the chief industries of South China, and 27 per cent. of the world's silk comes from China. Sericulture is the name given to the breeding and care of the silkworm. Cultivation of the mulberry tree is a necessary part of this craft, as silkworms are fed on mulberry leaves, but sericulture can only be carried on in places where the temperature can be kept above a certain level during the entire period of the worm's life. Under favourable conditions the women in South China expect to rear three successive generations of silkworms each year.

Bamboo is a natural produce of the land. The thickest stems of this strong and pliable plant serve to make the supports and beams of houses, while the split stem serves for thatching the roof and making beds and other necessary articles of furniture. Charcoal for heating braziers is made from the roots, and most of the accessories of the boatman's and fisherman's outfit are fashioned from bamboo, while the farmer uses it to make the water conduits of the irrigation system.

Cotton grows plentifully both in the south and in the north of China, as real heat for two months is sufficient to ripen the crop, and the plant requires a very moderate amount of moisture. Wherever cotton grows, hand-woven materials are plentiful, and the farmers grow indigo with which they dye the material in every shade of blue.

In North China wheat is grown widely, the best quality being the hard winter wheat, which is sown in the autumn in time to sprout before winter frost sets in. This is

EARLY MORNING MARKET AT A PEKING CITY GATE

THE FIVE-DRAGON BRIDGE IN THE FORBIDDEN CITY

[Page 48

PEKING. A CARVED MARBLE STAIRWAY

HOPING FOR A FREE RIDE

SELLING PEANUTS AT THE TEMPLE OF HEAVEN

FARMER'S WIFE OFF TO MARKET

reaped by the end of June, and is succeeded by autumn crops, which include millet, maize and sorghum. Last of all to be reaped is buckwheat, which, when all else fails through drought, is sometimes the only food of the North China farmer. Sorghum is a handsome plant which bears a coarse grain. It grows as tall as ten feet in height and is crowned with a splendid tuft bending under the weight of the grain which it bears. The crop supplies fodder for the transport beasts of the northern travel roads, and its leaves and stems are chopped and mixed with the grain in the manger.

The ground-nut or pea-nut is one of China's important and widely grown crops. The plant requires a light sandy soil on account of its peculiar growth. The flower appears above ground, but when it withers the stalk of the ovary bends down, elongates, and forces the pod underground, where the fruit forms and ripens. It is a prolific harvest, yielding thirty to thirty-eight bushels of nuts per acre. In parts of Honan where the land is too poor for general farming, the fields are covered with high mounds of the nuts at harvest time, and the village children are kept busy stripping them. All over China children eat roasted pea-nuts as in England they eat sweets, and in one laboratory in U.S.A. more than forty products have been made from the pea-nut, including salad-oil, nut-milk and margarine.

The growing of rice, the picking of tea and of cotton, sericulture and the manipulation of bamboo are all matters which demand the most meticulous care. It has been truly said, "The Chinese are sparing of all save trouble," but in that one respect they are regardless of expenditure. When the fields require weeding, when the shoots and leaves of the tea-plant must be picked and sorted, when the pods of cotton need to be harvested one by one at the exact moment when they burst and release the soft white substance which they enfold, women and children are expected to work indefatigably so that the man's strength will be conserved for heavier jobs. To make the earth yield the maximum of her increase is the dominant purpose of the agriculturist and his whole family.

The care of silkworms is a most exacting matter, for mulberry trees must be frequently stripped of their leaves to satisfy the increasing hunger of the rapidly growing grub. This also is one of the village women's and children's special industries. When the worm is nearly full size it has to be supplied with fresh food by day and by night, and there is no respite for those in charge. Thus the Chinese have become renowned for the occupations in which every member of the family has a share.

The soya bean (Glycine hispida) is very widely cultivated, especially in Manchuria, where an enormous acreage is devoted to its growth. The Chinese place great value on this bean as the basis of the famous soy sauce, which is a favourite condiment in Chinese cooking. It is also compressed into valuable fodder for horses, but in recent years scientific research has discovered many other uses for soya flour and for the milky curd which can be made from the bean. This latter has proved an excellent substitute for cow's milk in places where this is unobtainable, and is used in the infant welfare centres of Peking. Soya bean flour, being free of starch, can be taken by diabetic patients.

Tobacco (Nicotiana tabacum) was only introduced to China in 1530, but is now extensively cultivated both in the northern and southern provinces, and the sun-dried leaf forms a valuable line of export.

Medicinal plants are found in abundance, and the herbalist stalls are filled with a great variety. Rhubarb (Rheum palmatum) grows wild among rocky watercourses in both Szechwan and Kansu. Its bright reddish leaves are most decorative when they are caught by the sun's rays and show up as red spots in the yellow landscape.

One of the most important medicinal plants is liquorice (Glyrrhiza glabra). It grows prolifically in North China and in the oases of the Gobi Desert. The Chinese value it very highly. When it has been gathered the root is cut up, tied in bundles of varying lengths and stored round the courtyard.

Szechwan and Fukien provinces supply camphor (Cinnamomum camphora). The wood of the tree is distilled and the camphor is extracted and sold in blocks.

One of the most highly valued drugs obtained from China is ephedrine, which is now used so successfully in the treatment of asthma. It comes from a plant which grows in the Desert of Gobi, and has for long been used by native doctors.

There is one plant which has been very widely grown since the middle of the nineteenth century, when the Chinese began to sow fields of the opium poppy and its cultivation spread rapidly over the land. When the petals have fallen and the poppy head is bare, men and women go over the field scoring each head with a sharp knife. A thick dark brown substance oozes out, and this is the raw opium from which the drug is made. In many parts of China the sowing of the opium poppy is forbidden, but the habit of smoking or taking it in some other form is so difficult to eradicate that the government is often baffled in its efforts. In earlier days the Chinese did not smoke opium, and to this hour their name for it is " foreign smoke.'' In the eighteenth century the East India Company was exporting opium on a large scale, growing it in Bengal and selling it in China. In 1840 a dispute arose in Canton over opium smuggling, and the town was bombarded by British armed vessels, seized and forced to ransom itself. This is called the First Opium War. Later the Treaty of Nanking was signed, five Chinese ports were opened to foreign trade, extra-territoriality was introduced and China forced to pay a heavy indemnity. The opium trade went on, and in 1857 the Chinese authorities seized a ship in Canton waters which flew the British flag. The British claimed extrality for this ship, and when it was refused they seized Canton, and so the Second Opium War began. Further treaties were imposed on the Chinese, including that of Tientsin, which was signed in 1858. Gradually the British public came to know the facts of these wars, and public opinion was so roused to protest that the iniquitous opium traffic was brought to an end so far as Britain was concerned.

The vegetables found on Chinese markets are of excellent quality and endless variety. They include the egg-plant (aubergine), beans, carrots, turnips, ordinary and sweet potatoes, yams, cabbages, spinach, capsicum, sweet corn, lotus root, bamboo shoots and a great variety of pumpkins and marrows. There are also bean sprouts, which are produced by packing beans into large vats of water and allowing them to sprout in the dark. Strange to say that even where asparagus and Jerusalem artichokes are indigenous to the country, they are not eaten. Fruits vary according to latitude, but generally speaking grapes, peaches, apricots, apples, pears, nectarines, melons, persimmons and walnuts are of splendid quality in North and Central China, while oranges, pumeloes, pomegranates, pibas and lichees are found in the hotter places. In the most fertile parts of the central provinces it is claimed that forty different kinds of fruit are cultivated.

There is one oasis of the Gobi Desert called Turfan, where a small seedless grape grows in great profusion. The summer is intensely hot in that locality, and the vine-dressers build latticed drying-halls where the hot winds blow over the bunches of grapes and very quickly dry them into sultanas, which are carried by camel to China proper and to Siberia. The melons from some of the oases are of the finest quality, and the flesh is so firm that it can be cut into strips, dried and plaited into cakes, which travellers eat all through the winter on thirsty desert stages and in places where only bitter water is obtainable.

The salt trade is a monopoly of the Chinese Government, and no one may traffic in this commodity without paying a tax which was first imposed over four thousand years ago. The supply amounts to two million tons annually, and salt is therefore a great source of revenue to the State. It is found in several provinces, but the most important salt-springs are in Szechwan. While the borings are made to a depth of three thousand feet, sometimes through solid rock, the mouth of the well is often no wider than fourteen inches, and the brine is drawn up by five or more water buffaloes working on a wheel. Near the brine-springs there is an outlet of natural gas which supplies the heat needed for the evaporating process. Some of the salt wells are on the banks of the Yangtse, and when the river is low travellers can see the clouds of steam which arise from them, but when the water is high they are submerged. The captains of metal-built boats do not like to carry a cargo of salt, but the great wooden salt junks ply to and fro between Shanghai and the springs.

Further north in Shansi, Kansu and Sinkiang there are salt lakes and marshes. In south Shansi salt production is a very important industry, and near the evaporation tanks there are hillocks of glittering salt as high as a four-storied building, waiting to be carted away. On the borders of the Gobi Desert there are salt lakes which, at certain times of the year, fill up to the brim with brine and, when the water recedes, leave a fringe of salt all round the margin. Even in very desolate places there is a salt-gabelle station which collects a tax on every cartload which is taken away.

Antimony is a silvery-white, crystalline metal with a high lustre which is found in Hunan in quantities sufficient to supply the whole world's demand. Antimony is used in combination with other metals for forming alloys such as are used in making printers' type, white metal spoons and forks, and the lining of copper and brass saucepans.

Wolfram, also called tungsten, is found in the province of Kiangsi. It is used in the manufacture of steel, and until recent years was only to be found in China.

One of the greatest riches of North China is her deposits of coal. On the eastern border of Shansi is the most extensive bed of anthracite so far known in the world. The seams of coal lie very near the surface, and in many places the Chinese miners work them by the most primitive means, but in a few areas western machinery has been introduced and the output has consequently greatly increased. Much further north-west, in Kansu, there is both coal and anthracite of a very superior quality.

Mineral oil has long been used in its crude form in Sinkiang and in the province of Kansu, but in recent years oil-refining plant has been imported and local petrol is now being used by the motor traffic lines of the far north-west. There is undoubtedly great mineral wealth in China of which, so far, very little use has been made, and recent surveys are revealing hitherto unknown deposits of oil, coal, iron ore, lead, sulphur, gypsum and copper. China's mineral riches are still largely undeveloped, but with the pressing needs of warfare and the urgent demands made on her by all her allies, she is likely to become one of the world's most important centres for the export of raw materials.

CHAPTER IX

GOODS ON THE MOVE

THE transport of China's produce demands the ceaseless activity of an incredibly large number of people. The railway system is still very restricted, but each train is crowded with men and women of every class of society. A limited part of the country is now supplied with motor roads of varying quality, over which lorries and motor buses carry passengers and a small amount of goods, and these lorries are always piled high with bales of every description and carry as many passengers as can hang on to them. But what is conveyed by rail and motor transport is but a minute portion of China's colossal transport.

For thousands of years the traffic of the country has depended on the waterways in the south and on road traffic in the north. The waterways carry a seemingly endless stream of boats of every description, and the roads are filled with an equally endless line of carts, pack animals, wheelbarrows and pedestrians balancing an evenly divided load in two baskets slung on a pole across one shoulder. No country in the world has such a clever system of canalization as China, and every possible means of joining natural streams by means of artificial waterways has been used to the full. From the Sikiang to the Yangtse and via the Grand Canal up to Tientsin, agricultural produce is conveyed with the minimum output of strength and of expense.

In Central China there are hilly districts where passengers are carried in sedan-chairs by bearers, and where goods are transferred by coolies carrying loads across their shoulders. The men of Szechwan (Four Streams) province are renowned throughout China for their skill in this respect, and in that province there are many mountain roads which are roughly paved in stairways in order to give bearers a possible foot-hold. Trained men will carry burdens amounting to two hundred pounds up and down these difficult paths.

South China is covered with a network of rivers and canals, but North China is the land of dust and gullies. The kind of soil found there is called *loess,* which is a German word introduced to China by German geologists. The northern provinces merge into the sandy plains of Mongolia, where sandstorms are very frequent, and the fine sand which is lifted from the desert by these storms drifts southward and falls in a soft layer over the fields of North China. The result is a soil which is uniformly light yellow and is composed of a mixture of clay and sand which is friable and very absorbent. *Loess* crumbles easily and falls away so as to leave high jagged points of earth standing above deep ravines. It breaks in a vertical line, so that the country presents a remarkable aspect of peaks, chasms and gorges or canyons. The roads wear away very rapidly under the grind of traffic, and many of them have become deep gullies between *loess* cliffs rising twenty or thirty feet on either side, and are so narrow that two carts cannot pass each other. For one heavily laden cart to meet another in a narrow gully is an awkward predicament, so the carters have the habit of shouting and yelling as they go, to give warning to traffic ahead. Here and there the cliff has been cut away with spades so as to make a deep recess where a few carts can stand back and allow those coming in the other direction to get by.

The freight cart is a heavy, two-wheeled vehicle made of wood strengthened with iron. It is drawn by a team of five or more animals, but when it has to be dragged over a mountain pass many extra beasts are hitched to the axle by rope traces, for the cart, besides its own weight, carries

TAKING GOODS TO MARKET ON WHEELBARROWS

HARVESTING

WEIGHING BALES OF RAW COTTON

TERRACED RICE-FIELDS

more than one thousand pounds of merchandise. It is brakeless, but when coming downhill a log of wood is used to catch the wheel and check the speed. A rough matting awning makes a shelter for passengers from the scorching sun and from gales and blizzards. When crossing deserts a little wooden door is placed at the front of the cart to keep out the sand, but this travel cart supplies but poor comfort at the best.

In the larger cities there is a lighter vehicle called the Peking cart. It has a framework of wood or bamboo covered with dark blue cotton, and is drawn by one mule or horse. It is not intended to carry heavy loads or take long journeys. Wealthier homes keep one of these carts for personal use much as a family in the land of motors keeps a car.

In the villages where deep rivers have to be crossed bullock carts are used by the peasants. The wheels are about seven feet high, which enables passengers and goods to be taken across the river without getting wet. When the water is too deep the ox which drags the cart will swim to the opposite bank.

In North China river traffic is practically unknown, and freightage is consequently very much more expensive than in the south. While freight carts are drawn by teams of mules or horses, pack-mules and donkeys are in constant demand for conveying every kind of local produce, including grain and coal as well as loads of cloth, silk, paper, and a variety of manufactured articles from coastal areas. The only river which is navigable for boat traffic in North-West China is that portion of the Yellow River which flows through the province of Kansu between Lanchow and Paotow. All through the winter the river is frozen over, but in the spring it bursts its ice fetters with all the force of its released current, and after hurling many blocks of ice up its banks it carries the rest downstream until they are melted away in warmer climes. The people of Kansu have evolved a system of rafts resting on floats made from blown-out skins of sheep, goats or bullocks. The light board flooring of the raft is lifted above water level on these distended skins, and by this means heavy cargoes of goods, as well as many passengers, are conveyed for several weeks, by raft, to the railhead at Paotow. It is a dangerous way of transport, and the passengers' only sense of security rests on the ingenuity of the raftsman, who guides his craft with extraordinary skill among the cross-currents and eddies of the treacherous river.

In less mountainous regions of North China such as Hopeh, Shantung and Honan, the wheelbarrow is in great use. It is very heavily constructed, with a control wheel and a small platform on either side. Sometimes two travellers balance each other sitting on the platforms, but more often goods are carried carefully packed in loads of equal weight. A strap goes round the shoulders of the muscular barrow-man, and he holds the widely separated handles in each hand. It is work which exacts great expenditure of strength and also much skill in balancing the heavy, clumsy structure. When there is a following wind the barrow-man will fix a pole to either platform and make a sail by tying a cloth between the poles, and thus he lightens his job.

In the far north-west camel caravans are the favourite means of transport. The camel is the two-humped beast known as the Bactrian variety, whose humps form a natural and easy saddle. Camels are formed into caravans, in which several hundred laden beasts often walk in single file. They carry goods to and from Peking and Kashgar across Mongolia and Sinkiang, a journey which takes about five months at an average rate of three miles an hour. When perishable goods have to be moved quickly from one place to another, herds of small and inexpensive donkeys are used. These agile little creatures travel quickly over the thirty-mile stages, but as they are often overdriven they do not live long and may fall exhausted by the wayside. One man will drive a score of them, and he can guarantee to deliver the goods in fresh condition.

Nearer the Tibetan border the shaggy yak is the usual beast of burden. It can stand even the cold of the Tibetan heights on account of its thick hair, which reaches the ground all round its legs. The yak is a fearless swimmer and will take to the water even when rivers are in wild turbulent spate, always seeming to land safely on the other side, though frequently swept away for long distances by the current. The Tibetan drivers use the yak as a snow-plough, driving it over snow-blocked passes, then following behind in the path which it has cleared by brushing the snow aside with its tail.

CHAPTER X

LIFE IN NORTH CHINA VILLAGES

THE dress, the customs, the occupations and the food of a people are everywhere influenced by climatic and geographical conditions. It would be difficult to find two countries in greater contrast with each other, as regards soil and climate, than are North and South China, yet their inhabitants have this in common, that in both places the overwhelming majority of the people are agriculturists, for China reckons that over eighty per cent. of her inhabitants are engaged in farming.

The northerner is taller, less talkative and less excitable than the southerner, but both have the same physical characteristics of high cheek-bones, flattened nose, straight black hair and slanting eyes, and mentally the same determination to overcome difficulties and to turn to best use every advantage that the narrow circumstances of life afford them.

In the central area the annual rainfall registers about forty-five inches, and the winter temperature is lower than would be expected in England on a rather chilly spring day, while the summer heat is intense, but both cold and heat are made much harder to bear by the constant moisture of the air. In the very south of China, midwinter is as warm as an English summer, and the summer temperature is correspondingly high. Further north the climate is extremely dry and very sunny, with much wider difference between winter and summer temperatures. In summer the thermometer goes up to 110° F., and in winter it falls to about twelve degrees below zero. There is a rainy season in July and August, but frequently very little rain falls during the remainder of the year.

The villages of North China are not colourful because the houses are made of mud bricks which are identical in colour with the *loess* soil. These bricks are made from mud, which is mixed to the right consistency, then pressed into a wooden frame, turned out in the form of a large brick and dried by sun heat. The poorest houses are mere hovels, and cave dwellings are popular. Wherever there is a *loess* hill, the villagers hollow caves from its side and live in them with considerable comfort, because they are easily warmed in the winter and form a very cool shelter from the burning sun in summer. The caves are often built tier above tier, with small paths leading from one level terrace to another. It is not unusual to see the smoke coming from a mud chimney pot at the edge of a field or threshing floor, and this just shows that the land under foot has been excavated and that the farmer and his family are living in caves, the roof of which is the field that he cultivates.

The cave is often thirty feet deep. It has one window

in which there is paper instead of glass. Under the window there is a large platform about three feet high made of mud bricks. It is called a *kang*. During the day the women sit on the *kang* and do their work, eat their meals and receive callers. It is hollow, and at one end it has a stove from which the hot air travels through a flue to a chimney which is at the other end. In cold weather the *kang* is always kept warm, and at night it provides sleeping space for the family. Further down the cave is a kitchen table, which is a very large smooth board on which flour and water paste is rolled out for the family food. When the sheet of paste is almost as thin as paper it is cut into fine strips with a heavy chopper, thrown into a cauldron of boiling water and vegetables, ladled into bowls and eaten with chopsticks. The depths of the cave are used as a store-room for grain, pickled vegetables, dried capsicum, hemp-seed oil and home-made vinegar. A loom and a spinning-wheel generally stand on the *kang,* and even small children will spin very cleverly while their mothers and elder sisters weave homespun cloth of which to make clothes and shoes for the family. Outside the cave door is a level space often used as a threshing-floor, and on it is a mill to which a mule or donkey is harnessed for grinding flour.

The livestock of the small landowner consists in a donkey, a pig, half-a-dozen sheep and a few fowls. The richer man has, in addition, mules, bullocks, and a large flock of sheep and goats. Mutton and fowl are used for food, but bullocks and heifers are too valuable to be slaughtered. They are kept for ploughing and for drawing bullock-carts; nor are the village cows usually milked, as few Chinese care for milk, butter or cheese. The only pasture is in hilly places where patches of land are useless for cultivation, but sheep also nibble down the autumn-sown wheat, and the leaves of trees are swept up and stored to help them through the lean winter months. These sheep belong to the broad-tailed breed which stores fat in the tail during the plentiful season, and gradually absorbs it in times of scarcity.

In order to increase the acreage of arable land farmers cut the crumbling hillside into a series of terraces, each fortified by a carefully strengthened bank. In this way a steep hill sloping from a *loess* peak can be brought under cultivation. In those parts land is spoken of as " dry land " and " watered land," the former depending on rain and snow, and the latter on irrigation. According to rural law each farmer has an exactly calculated share of the available water supply which flows through his own channel for a certain length of time and is then diverted to his neighbour's land. The system entails a great deal of labour, but if a matter is considered important, the Chinese never suggest that it is too much trouble.

As a result of irrigation, in the northern provinces two successive crops are reaped each summer, and in the south the industrious farmer will raise three crops of rice in one year. In many mountain villages in North China water is so scarce that it has to be fetched from a stream which is a mile away. Once each day a donkey is laden with wooden panniers and driven to the stream, where they are filled, and the family has to reduce its use of water to this meagre supply. Only on the few days of the year when clouds collect and bring abundant rain do such villages know the luxury of an adequate supply.

Each son when he marries brings his bride home to the family farm, where she is expected to take her full share in community work. The men of the household excavate a fresh cave for each bridal pair, and there the conditions of life which have been those of the parents are carried on to the younger generation.

In each hamlet there is a temple dedicated to the worship of gods made of plaster or wood. At the entrance there is usually a representation of two fierce armed warriors, and further in are hideous and cruel-looking idols. In the courtyard there is often a tree which is more than a century old, with wide-spreading branches reaching right across from one shrine to the other. Within the shrines there may be figures of the Buddha, or there may be tablets which show it to be a Confucian temple. There is always a burner filled with the dust of burned incense sticks, and here the village people come on stated days to offer homage to their own hand-made gods.

When the longed-for rainy season is a failure and the wheat is scorching in the fields, the villagers go to the temple, take away the image of a god, and carry him in procession under the blazing midday sunshine, that he too may have a taste of its fierceness, and remember to send the rain. In the south, where excessive rain is more often the farmer's problem, the villagers carry a jar of rain-water up to the hills where the Water Dragon lives, in order to bring it to his notice that some drier weather would be a great help to the farmers on the plain.

Every man devotes a corner of his land to be the family graveyard. The mounds which mark the spot are carefully repaired once every year at the spring festival of Clear Brightness. Cypress trees are planted to throw a shade over the graves and to fill the air with their pungent fragrance; and here the dead are remembered as widows mourn their husbands and orphans wail for their parents.

CHAPTER XI

LIFE IN SOUTH CHINA VILLAGES

VILLAGE life in Central and in South China is different in many respects from that in the northern provinces. Instead of dryness there is a superabundance of rain, of rivers and of canals. Instead of relying on a mule, a donkey or a bullock for tilling the land and for transporting farm produce, most families in the south have a boat and many own a water-buffalo. The farmer himself uses this beast for field work, but the children of the family take it to the river or the pond for its daily relaxation of wallowing in the water.

As the farmer's boy grows older and stronger much hard work awaits him, and he has but little opportunity of any steady school life. In the north the cold winter months call a halt on farm work, and for a winter term of six months the boy can apply himself to learning in the village school, but in the south the three consecutive sowings and reapings of the rice crops allow but little leisure to the farmer himself or to any member of his family. As soon as he is old enough the boy learns to stand for long hours in a flooded rice field, stooping down to push each of the seedlings which he is transplanting deep into the ooze. The irrigation of the land requires constant attention, as the water is mainly controlled by the building up or breaking down of mud dykes through which it reaches the fields. There are also various contrivances for forcing water uphill by means of tread-pumps, and by working these he strengthens his muscles until he can endure the strain of working almost incessantly from dawn till dark. In many small holdings there is no buffalo, and all the ploughing, as

REAPING THE RICE HARVEST

GIRLS IN A POPPY FIELD

BAMBOO GROVE

well as the reaping and threshing, is done by hand. After the last crop of rice has been cut the fields are re-ploughed and vegetables of many kinds are sown. These are a very welcome addition to the food, but nothing is allowed to hold up land-space when the rice-growing season begins and the young plants in the seed-beds are ready to be transplanted. Everything is cleared away to make room for the first main crop of the year.

Most families rear a few sheep, but they can never be allowed outside the sheds where they live, as there are no fences and hedges to divide the holdings, and they would inevitably damage the crops. Young children collect fodder wherever there is grass to cut, and the sheep are fed in the huts.

Each household tries to keep a few pigs, in fact the ideograph which represents the word " home " is formed of a roof with a pig under it. As many fowls as can scratch a living for themselves are encouraged to do so. Village folk live sparingly on plain boiled rice with the addition of small dishes of fish, pork, fowl and highly flavoured pickles, and it is considered very wrong to waste food, or even to leave a few grains of rice at the bottom of the bowl. Cooking-pots and serving-dishes are carefully scraped, and any remaining food is saved for another meal.

The farmer's home is usually built round three sides of a square courtyard, which the family more or less shares with pigs, hens and the water-buffalo. Besides living-room and kitchen, there are various storehouses and sheds. The better buildings are tiled and the poorer are thatched with rice straw. The eaves are low and wide, serving to protect the papered windows from rain, and also to shade the rooms from scorching sun. They also ensure a dry passage round the courtyard so that the family can move from room to room without being drenched by the rain. An open-air mud cooking-stove is often in use during very hot weather.

Besides a very large preponderance of farmers the village has craftsmen, principally workers in bamboo or in silk, shopkeepers and fishermen. In the most densely inhabited areas there are as many as two thousand inhabitants per square mile, and it requires a very sustained effort to feed so many from the land. In North China the population is reckoned at about 67 per square mile, and up in some of the far north-west dependencies it is only about 2 per square mile.

CHAPTER XII

LIFE ON THE WATERWAYS

THERE are many millions of Chinese who are born, brought up and spend the whole of their life on a river boat. The girls of the family, at marriage, are merely transferred to the boat on which the bridegroom lives, and there they bring up their own children, and will only finally leave their little craft when their bodies are carried ashore and buried by the riverside.

The ordinary river boat is flat-bottomed and square at each end. The middle of the deck is covered with plaited bamboo matting and forms the cabin which is hired by passengers, who are always referred to as " guests." The front of the boat is reserved for the rowers, who stand to propel the boat. When there is a strong current and the likelihood of rapids, a crew of several hired men will be needed to man the oars, and hard work is expected of them all through the day, but at night the boat is tied up and all lie down to sleep till daylight.

The rowers know by the look of the water when they are nearing a rapid, and as they come close the roaring of the waves is an alarming note of danger. Each rower watches for the line of surf which will carry the boat on to the dangerous down-pouring flood, and each one is alert and tense to his own part of guiding the boat to safety. For the next few moments the waters around the little craft boil and foam and toss. Then the danger is over, the boat again floats in the quiet waters, and everyone relaxes with a sigh of relief. The river folk are accustomed to facing such perils, but they never lose the sense of danger at the moment of shooting the rapids, because they have known so many families to be drowned in that turbulent water. It is because of this that, before starting on the journey, they sacrifice a hen and burn some sticks of incense in the prow of the boat in order to propitiate the river god.

The waterways present many interesting and curious sights. There are fishermen who have trained otters to work for them by diving and bringing back fish in their mouths, which they drop into a jar full of water. Others sit in a boat with a dozen birds called cormorants perched on the edge of the craft to help in the fishing. At a signal the birds will dive and bring back the fish in their mouths, but their necks are encircled with a ring to prevent them from swallowing the fish which they have caught.

The boatman's family has very small quarters in which to live, cook and sleep, but they are all very little under cover and live an open-air life of hard work, which makes them strong and healthy. Boat life is dangerous for a venturesome toddler, so in babyhood it is safely tied to its mother's back, and when it begins to run about a block of wood or bamboo is fastened to its body to keep it afloat whenever it falls overboard. There is no schooling for the river-folk children with their mobile life, but plenty of work for all, and at the age of five they are already learning to steer, to coil ropes, to guard the boat from thieves and to help in innumerable ways. Small punts carry local produce, houseboats will convey a party of travellers for several weeks' river journey, and the square-prowed ocean junks are a beautiful sight as, with all sails set, they fly before the wind. These usually have great eyes painted on the prow that they may see their way over the ocean track. Most of them are wind-driven, but some are propelled by great paddle-wheels in the stern which are turned by the tread of gangs of coolies.

On the waterways, whenever there is anything to cause a congestion of traffic, the number of boats becomes so great that an active boy can go for miles by leaping from boat to boat without ever touching land. In the busy waterside towns shoppers use boats to ferry from one place to another, and school-children are collected and deposited at their various schools by the boatmen.

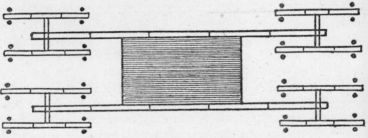

Shaded area is weight : hollow lines are bamboo poles : each dot is a man.

Canton has one of the largest boat populations of China, and though some families have become wealthy and live on gaily painted junks, they still remain a class apart and do not intermarry with land folk. At all the wharfs of important towns gangs of coolies work daily at lading and unlading cargo. They carry very skilfully, and by using strong bamboo poles they shift great weights by man-power only. The accompanying diagram shows how thirty-two men will co-ordinate their strength to move one heavy object without getting in each other's way. In order to do this they move and act in perfect harmony, and to ensure this co-operation they emit a rhythmic sound which is very melodious and helps to regulate their movements. No one who has visited a Chinese port will ever forget the low monotone uttered by coolie teams at work.

CHAPTER XIII

LIFE IN TOWNS

THE " Hundred Families People " have always been classified according to a very sensible and democratic order of society. The highest class was that of scholarship, next in order came the agriculturist, then the artisan, and below these stood the merchant. The soldier came last in the social scale. According to ancient Chinese State law, " there is no such thing as being born noble," but universal respect for learning ordains that everyone who is well-educated should form part of the upper class. Of the remaining divisions the agriculturist stood highest because he is producer of the nation's food, the artisan next, for he converts raw material into useful articles, the merchant was below him as a mere distributor of goods, and least worthy of all was the military class, for soldiers destroy life and property which others have laboriously built up. Modern warfare has raised the status of the army, but only a few years ago it was still held in scorn, and while every father coveted a scholar son he was ashamed if his son joined the military.

Village life in China exalts the farmer, but among town-dwellers business life is attractive because it brings in money and the luxury which money commands. A business street in an inland town is a very gay sight. The shops are rather like stalls, for the counter is used to separate the shop from the street, and many customers prefer to sit on narrow benches which are placed on the side-walk and buy what they want without going inside. As soon as a customer begins to examine the goods, an apprentice places a small cup of straw-coloured tea at his elbow that he may sip it during the lengthy business of bargaining prices. No one requires either milk or sugar, and the tea is called '' green tea '' as distinguished from the '' red tea '' that westerners use.

The shop frontage is decorated with scarlet, blue or green banners on which are written the merchant's name, the sign of the shop and mottoes which are drawn from old books. When meal-time comes the half-dozen apprentices lay a table just inside the counter and sit down to a meal of bread or rice with several dishes of vegetables cooked with mutton, fowl or fish. The master of the establishment sits a little to one side smoking a pipe with a bamboo stem three feet long and a tiny bowl which only holds a pinch of tobacco, and which he refills after taking three or four puffs. The back door of the shop opens on to a square courtyard, in which are his store-rooms and where he lives with his wife and children.

Shops which sell some particular line of goods are generally assembled in one street, and they often give it a name: Shoemaker Street, Rope-maker's Alley, Pawnbroker Lane, Jade Street and Lacquer Street are localities which speak for themselves, but of all the business houses none is stocked with richer or more fascinating goods than the shops of the silk merchants' quarter. Here the buyers always go inside, and both shopkeeper and customer prepare for a long sitting. It may be that a daughter is shortly to be married, and her mother has come with a couple of women relatives to help her select the trousseau silks. The wedding clothes must all be made of scarlet, but there must also be twenty summer dresses in delicate shades of pale grey, ivory white, duck-egg, turquoise blue and rose-pink, while the same number of wadded winter gowns will be made of heavy brocades in darker colours. Her coats will be tailored with fur linings and brocade covers, and the trousseau must include at least a dozen wadded quilts made up of patterned silks of the most elaborate designs.

In the course of half an hour the counter is covered with a gorgeous display of magnificent silk materials in every colour and shade, but no purchase is made without careful computation as to quality and the exact amount required. There is no hurry or bustle and no mistakes occur, for these ladies are most experienced buyers and judge so well of respective values that, by the time the bargaining is through, the shopkeeper will only have made his legitimate profit on the transaction.

Down each side of the street numbers of artisans work at their varied crafts. Shoemakers are numerous, for Chinese men like to wear heelless black cloth shoes which are inexpensive but do not last long. The tailor does his work in the open, and it is fascinating to watch him as, by means of a taut string and a bag of powdered chalk, he sketches a diagram on the cloth and cuts the garment with perfect precision according to its intersecting lines. In another shop frontage three men have strapped themselves to a strong bar of wood, and with bare feet they tread sheep's or goat's hair into thick felt. When their work is done they will have produced the felt mats for rich people's *kangs* and cheap round felt caps with ear-tabs for village labourers who are out of doors in all weathers. There is one dingy shop standing back from the street which seems full of small stoves built from mud. All the stoves are covered with boiling kettles, and this is a " boiling-water shop." Fuel is often scarce and heating water is troublesome, so if a friend calls it is simple and economical to take a pot to the boiling-water shop and make the tea there. Near the shop there are always children with brimming teapots in their hands, running so as to get home before the tea is cold.

The pawnbroker has a peculiar frontage, for his shop entrance is built up so that all transactions are discussed over the top of a boarding which is as high as the customer's head. It is not only the poor man who comes to the pawnbroker with a garment to pledge, but there are many among the well-to-do who bring their best clothes to be stored there when not required, and who make a practice of laying up a fur coat during the summer and a midsummer garment during the winter.

The roadway of the main streets is always encumbered with vendors who carry their goods balanced across one shoulder. The itinerant barber is on the look-out for a man who wants a shave, and as soon as he gets a sign from someone he produces stool, towel and razor and shaves his customer in the middle of all the hurly-burly of the street. There is always a hungry man to shout at the mobile food-seller, who instantly slips the trays of food from his shoulder and begins to make ready a simple and appetizing meal. A brazier keeps the chitterling broth boiling, and the bean-flour shape, which we call blancmange, is cut in fine strips and served with vinegar and a dusting of cayenne.

Another vendor of eatables advertises the cheapness of his goods by calling out: " Picked up wheat and a demon turned the mill," which means " It cost me little and yours will be the gain," but for all that his first price will not be a small one, and the buyer will have to beat him down if he is going to buy cheap.

If the town is near a river or a canal, there will be a ceaseless stream of water-carriers bringing pails of soft river water to housewives busy with the family wash. The single file of laden carriers moves with a rhythmic jog-trot and a monotonous cry which helps to keep the line moving at an

MAN WITH GOAT-SKIN RAFT KEPT FOR USE ON THE SWIFT-FLOWING
YELLOW RIVER

BAMBOO RAFT IN SOUTH CHINA

[Page 72

A TYPICAL CITY PASSENGER CART

A TYPICAL FERRY BOAT

even pace, and as they go they pass the swifter line of men with empty buckets who wend their way back to the riverside to dip and fill their pails again, then carry them back through the crowded thoroughfare.

The streets of large towns for all the hours between sunrise and sunset are filled with a noisy crowd of men, each of whom is intent on his own business, and whose dominant thought is how he can earn a living and supply his family with food for another day.

CHAPTER XIV

CHINA'S DEPENDENCIES

CHINA'S dependencies form her land frontier from northwest to north-east. They include Tibet, Sinkiang, Mongolia and Manchuria, and beyond Manchuria lies Korea, which was once counted among the dependencies. Some of these provinces have been seized by outside powers, which now control them, while others exercise a larger or smaller degree of independence.

The first to be lost to China was Korea, a peninsula about six hundred miles long extending southward from Manchuria. The seaboard is fringed by a line of over two hundred volcanic islands, of which about one hundred and thirty are inhabited. Some of them are mere masses of volcanic rock rising to an altitude of two thousand feet. Korea is very little smaller than Great Britain, and has an excellent climate which only becomes hot and surcharged with humidity for about three months of the year. The population, which numbers about twenty million, is of the Mongolian race. Their language is different in structure from the Chinese, for it is polysyllabic and has an alphabet

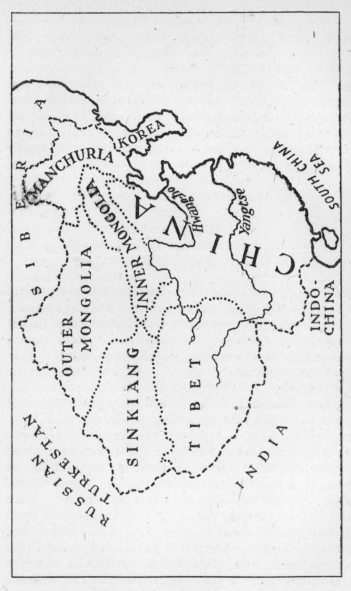

CHINA'S DEPENDENCIES AND FRONTIERS

composed of eleven vowels and fourteen consonants. The land is fertile in grain, cotton and silk, and has valuable deposits of coal and iron.

Until 1895 Korea was under Chinese rule, but from that time there were constant political difficulties, and during the Russo-Japanese war which broke out in 1904 she became the battlefield of contending nations. When peace was concluded she was granted a considerable measure of independence, and this she enjoyed for some years. Korea was, however, in the dangerous position of a small and undefended nation surrounded by powerful neighbours who might at any time use her territory as a base for attack on an enemy. The King of Korea exercised the right of independent sovereignty until 1910, when he ceded his rights to the Emperor of Japan.

Mongolia is a vast territory of 130,000 square miles, which is divided into Inner and Outer Mongolia, the former of which touches China and the latter of which borders Siberia. Mongolia is sparsely populated, and agriculture is impossible except in a few areas. The whole country is a plateau from three to five thousand feet above sea level. The climate is hot and dry in the summer and intensely cold during the winter. Its dryness is largely due to the wall of mountains on the east and south boundary which are called Khingan, and which shut out the moist winds. Consequently Mongolia has one of the driest climates in the world. It has vast stretches of grassland, and on the borders of the mountains trees and water are found in abundance, but there are wide expanses of sandy waste. The people are nomadic, live in felt tents and move from place to place seeking pasture for their flocks. The trade-routes of Mongolia are mainly caravan camel tracks, but Kwei-hwa-cheng in north Shansi is now connected both with Urga and with Hami by motor traffic. The Great Wall was originally intended to divide Mongolia from China in days when the

Mongols were great warriors and a source of terror to the Chinese. Now they show very little warlike spirit, but herd their cattle and shun intercourse with other nations, whom they know to be more astute in worldly affairs than they are themselves.

China was the governing power in Mongolia until a few years ago, and local administration was carried out under the supervision of Chinese officials. In 1911, during the Chinese revolution, Outer Mongolia tried to secure its independence. It has now adopted a Soviet form of government, and is under treaty of protection by the U.S.S.R. Inner Mongolia remains Chinese, but has suffered invasion by Japan on the eastern side.

Manchuria lies on the north-east of China. It is a large country, eight hundred miles long and five hundred miles wide, and is divided politically into three provinces. It touches China and Mongolia on the west and Siberia on the north and east. The climate is very dry and presents extremes of heat and cold, the winter temperature ranging from ten to twenty degrees below zero. Manchuria has a very fertile soil, and many of the mountains are covered with forests. It has great mineral wealth and many precious stones are found there. Of recent years it has become famous as the land of the soy bean. During the last half-century Manchuria has passed through times of great political difficulty. At the close of the nineteenth century she was claimed by Russia as a natural sphere of influence. This aggressive attitude led to war between Japan and Russia, and at the close of the war (1895), when Russia was beaten, the Japanese handed Manchuria over to China. From that time and until 1907 it was governed from Peking as a separate possession, after which it was converted into a Viceroyalty with the Viceroy's seat at Moukden, the capital. The last dynasty of the Imperial Government was Manchurian. It came into power at the close of the sixteenth century, and the last Emperor, who was a mere child, abdicated in 1912 on the proclamation of the Chinese Republic. His dynastic title was Hsuan Tung, and he is still alive, but is now known as Pu-yi. He lives at Moukden as nominal head of the Japanese puppet government of Manchuria.

About twenty years after handing the country over to China, Japan began to show by a series of aggressive incidents that she herself wished to occupy Manchuria. She landed successive parties of troops, seized the railways and exercised increasingly widespread control. Finally, in 1937, fighting broke out near Peiping and marked the beginning of the long war between China and Japan.

The land of Tibet is often spoken of as the land of mystery. The reason for this is doubtless its inaccessibility and political barriers which make it impossible for Europeans to travel freely within its borders. The population is reckoned to be three to four million people, and their land is seven times the size of England, Scotland and Ireland combined. Tibet is the highest country in the world, and is a land of great mountain ranges and high plateaux. The peaks which stand out from the Himalayan range are as high as 24,600 feet, and the passes through the mountains rise to 19,000 feet. The strain on the hearts of men and beasts when travelling at these altitudes is tremendous, and only those caravan men who are accustomed to the journey are prepared to take their ponies over the steep roads. The climate of the highest country in the world is, as would be expected, intensely cold, and the bitterness of this is made worse by terrific winds which blow violently for most of the year.

The products of Tibet include gold, and some of the temple roofs are overlaid with gold leaf. The land is probably very rich in minerals but has never been surveyed, and Tibetans barter pelts, gold and precious stones for grain and cloth. The yak is the beast of burden and supplies the people with milk. It is a most valuable creature, reliable and sure-footed, and it will brush away the snow from the mountain passes with its great tail and so prepare a way for the caravans to pass over. The flowers of Tibet are very fine, and on the plateaux every kind of alpine flora can be seen—gentians, edelweiss, orchids and every variety of rhododendron. Two plants which are indigenous to Tibet are the famous blue poppy and black clematis. This is the land where Mount Everest stands, that great and mighty mountain peak which has so far defied every attempt man has made to reach its summit. Doubtless some day it will be scaled, but until then it remains a challenge to mountaineers.

Tibet is under the political control of China, but the government is really in the hands of the Dalai Lama, who is the spiritual head, and the Panchan Lama, who is the political head. Local chiefs rule over the people, who are nomads, and each family will give one son to temple service. He lives with other priests in a lamasery, where religious rites are carried on and where the people all gather together at times of festival. The people of Tibet are friendly when left to themselves, but are fearful of intrusion by outside powers. The Chinese are not liked by them, and missions from the Governments of England and Russia have also been viewed with suspicion in Lhasa, although many trade agreements have been concluded. Tibet must finally decide with which power she will establish friendly political relations, but not until the lama system is broken can her people be free to take a part in the government of their country or to have intercourse with other lands. The ignorance in which they are kept, their illiteracy and their superstition are not likely to disappear until the power of the ecclesiastical hierarchy is broken.

The territory now called Sinkiang (New Dominion) has

been of vital importance to China ever since earliest times.
For many centuries before she opened up communication by
sea with other lands, China was using the trade-routes of
Central Asia to carry her produce to the most distant
markets. Camel caravan leaders were familiar, through
constant coming and going, with every possible desert track,
and only warfare interrupted their business. On many
occasions China was forced to send armies to that far-away
north-west area, but it was always for the purpose of
keeping trade-routes open between herself and the West.

The province of Sinkiang covers half-a-million square
miles, and is bordered on the north by Siberia, on the east
by Mongolia, on the south by China proper and Tibet, and
on the west by Russian Turkestan, the Pamirs, and the
Himalayan range, which separates her from India. She is
traversed from east to west by a high range of mountains
called the Tien Shan (Heavenly Mountains), and she
encloses the greater portion of the Deserts of Gobi and Lob.
Much of the land is very flat, with a depression in the
Turfan area which is about five hundred feet below sea
level. Streams which flow down from the glaciers and
snowfields of the high mountains form oases, and wherever
irrigation is possible the land is extremely fertile. The
principal products are grain (including rice), cotton, sheep
and lamb-skins, and fruit which is exported in the form
of sultanas, dried apricots and dried plums. The
melons which are grown in certain oases are unequalled
in quality.

Men of many different nationalities overran Sinkiang in
the course of the centuries, and each left behind some
national strain. At the present time many languages are
spoken there, and men of varying nationalities and differing
religious customs live in close proximity in the oases towns,
yet without mixing and with very little intermarriage or
intercourse apart from necessary business dealings.

Politically the country belongs to China, and all public and government offices are controlled by Chinese officials. The Turki and Tatar people, however, constitute a majority of the inhabitants; they are Moslems and speak Tatar dialects which vary according to the locality.

CHAPTER XV

CHINESE INVENTIONS

MANY things of which we make constant use were first discovered by the Chinese, but they often handled their knowledge in a simple and unscientific way. On the whole it can be said that discoveries which could be developed by craftsmen's skill and by means of patience and toil reached the point of perfection in their hands, while other inventions which demanded the application of scientific knowledge remained in an elementary stage until the western nations carried them forward.

Ancient records of Chinese history going back to over one thousand years B.C. relate that an embassy came from the lands south of the mountains, bringing offerings of ivory, spices, and other precious articles to the ruler of China. He sent them back laden with presents and, hearing that they were anxious lest they lose their way on the return journey, he told them not to worry as he could help them in the matter. When they left he produced chariots for the journey, and in front of each one was a small iron figure of a man with hand outstretched. The hand, he told them, would always point south, and if they followed it would safely guide them home. This story has come down in legendary form, but it shows clearly that the Chinese had discovered the means of making a magnetic needle. To

NORTH CHINA FARMERS WITH SAILING WHEELBARROWS

MILLING GRAIN IN A CHINESE COURTYARD

[Page 80

AERIAL VIEW OF THE LOESS REGION

CAVE-DWELLINGS IN SHANSI

GULLY THROUGH A LOESS REGION

PLOUGHING A FLOODED RICE-FIELD
WOMEN PREPARING RICE-SEEDLINGS FOR TRANSPLANTING

this day the compass in China is called the " south-pointing needle."

The art of paper-making was discovered by the Chinese before the time of Christ, and they still hold their own as adepts in that industry. In earlier times they wrote on thin strips of bamboo or wood, but Chinese writing quickly became an artistic achievement when some unknown person thought of separating the fibre of rags, hemp, or the foliage of certain wild plants and depositing the fibrous mass on a fine sieve under water.

In most Chinese villages the paper-maker can still be seen at work, raising the hand-made sieve from the tank of water and, with marvellous dexterity, lifting the small square sheet of wet paper and laying it against a white-washed wall to dry in the sun.

The invention of printing is also due to the Chinese, who were the first people to cut wood blocks. A piece of polished wood, the size of two pages of a book, on which raised ideographs were cut, was brushed over with ink made from oil and lampblack, then pressed evenly on a sheet of smooth paper and, being lifted, left a clear impress behind. Each sheet was then folded in two, back to back, and all were stitched together by hand in right order, and so the first book came into being. Chinese books are very often made up in this manner at the present time. Printing on one side of the sheet only and folding it with the print outside enables bookbinders to use very thin and inexpensive paper.

The Chinese have a real talent for finance, and travellers of the Middle Ages brought back a report to Europe that in China a printed slip of paper was equivalent to hard cash. So the use of paper money was gradually introduced to the western world until it has become general, but its invention is due to the Chinese. All western countries now use a financial system based on what is called the Bill of

Exchange, by means of which money can be drawn by a traveller at various points of his journey and at stated times. It is a very useful system, and the Chinese invented it about thirteen hundred years ago, long before we had any banking system at all. They also called it by a much more attractive name than Bill of Exchange —they called it '' Flying Money,'' because when a business man started out on a long journey in the course of which he would require to use a great deal of money, he found that by this arrangement, when he reached a distant town, the money had got there ahead of him, and was awaiting his arrival. '' This is Fei-chien (Flying Money),'' he said, and so the name became general.

One of the epoch-making inventions of the Chinese was the making of porcelain. We still speak of anything of the kind as china because the whole industry was invented, developed and perfected by the Chinese. They had made pottery for many centuries previously and learnt how to bake it, but in the seventh century it was discovered that by mixing a fine white clay with sand and powdered stone, sifted and purified, the smooth white paste which emerged could be fired, and the result was something finer and whiter than any previously known ware. The Chinese were very soon producing beautiful vases, dishes and figures such as we see in our museums at the present day. They learnt to tint glazes with beautiful colourings, from the palest grey and duck-egg green to rich yellow, purple and blood-red. They also decorated vases, teapots and cups with quotations from the classics written in small delicate ideographs which harmonized with the twigs and tendrils of the flower scheme. Porcelain which was made for the Imperial household was often ornamented with dragon designs, and only the Imperial porcelain might have five claws to the dragon. At one time there were one million workers employed at the Imperial porcelain factories.

The discovery of how to use saltpetre led both to the making of fireworks and crackers, and of gunpowder and explosives. It was the Chinese who made the first experiments in what we call pyrotechnics, but they only used the explosive qualities of the mixture for harmless though gorgeous displays of fireworks, whereas the western nations turned the discovery into the channel of making ammunition for purposes of warfare.

About 2700 B.C. the Emperor's wife Lei-tzu is believed to have discovered how to unwind the filaments of a cocoon, draw them into one thread and weave it into the fabric which we call silk. The insect which made this cocoon was, of course, the silkworm, which, if suitably fed and protected from cold, will give a very large yield of silk thread. For long centuries the Chinese had a monopoly of silken goods, and they sent them by camel caravan across the Gobi Desert to Rome long before the Christian era. The technique of sericulture is very ancient, but it is still practised in its original form in innumerable towns and villages of China. Groves of mulberry trees are necessary to the industry, for from the time when the worm hatches from its egg it must be sufficiently and suitably fed. The grubs grow very rapidly, and are kept on wide trays which hold the mulberry leaves conveniently. At the moment when all the worms want to spin a cocoon they become restless and try to get away from the tray. They must then be supplied with twigs and, fastening on to these, they spin out a thread with which they cover their own bodies until all there is to be seen is a number of soft, resisting, light yellow cocoons. If the worm were allowed to live it would come out a moth, but each cocoon is plunged into boiling water and the larva dies. Then the women and girls draw out the silk thread, which, it is said, may be a thousand yards long, and must, if possible, be unbroken. A garment woven from this perfectly pure silk can be folded and kept for centuries without cutting at the folds.

Co-operative movements are now coming to the help of the village silk industry. They supply sheets of eggs guaranteed free of disease and set up silk-winding machinery which draws the thread at more even pressure than can be insured by hand, and therefore diminishes the risk of breaking the filament. Thanks to scientific investigation the output of China's silk industry is likely to be greatly increased.

China has been credited with endless discoveries, and it is certain that some of the most modern inventions had their origin in a Chinese notion. " There is nothing new under the sun " said Solomon the wise, and in the ninth century A.D. a cart was used in China to which a drum was attached which, after a certain number of revolutions of the wheel, was struck by a mechanical device. This was the first speedometer, but the Chinese name was " measure-mile-drum-cart."

CHAPTER XVI

WHAT IS THAT?

ONE of the first sentences learnt by a newcomer is " Na shi shen-mo? "—" What is that?" because he soon finds that it is only by means of asking questions and listening to the answers that he can learn what is going on, and what is the meaning of the various things he sees around him in a land which is so unlike his own.

The main streets of cities, the entrance to villages, and even the country roads of China are spanned by handsome ornamental archways raised in memory of outstanding citizens. They always bear two ideographs meaning " By

Imperial Decree," for they might only be erected by permission of the Emperor. They often commemorate some act of virtue which specially appeals to the Chinese sense of decorum, such as a family which lived in harmony and remained undivided for four or five generations, or the honour due to a woman who was widowed in her youth but would never re-marry, or they may commemorate the virtue of officials who were blameless in the discharge of their duties. All these are counted worthy to have their names handed down to posterity, and the archway which bears the inscription is called a *Pai-lou,* which means " Erection bearing a tablet."

Having satisfied his curiosity regarding the *Pai-lou,* he will next ask about a man sitting before a tray which is laden with many kinds of money. This, he is told, is the money-changer, who deals in coppers, silver dollars and paper notes. There are long strings of one thousand cash which are threaded through a square hole in the centre of each round coin, and those who are philosophically minded say that every cash is a symbol of the square earth set in the midst of a round Universe. There are also ten-cash pieces which are larger and are not pierced with a hole, so cannot be strung together; these are wrapped up in paper parcels of a hundred coins. Then there is lump silver, which has been a favourite form of currency with business men. It is melted down by the silversmith in the form of " shoes " or blocks of varying size, and a one-ounce shoe is called a *tael.* When a merchant wants change for lump silver the money-changer chips a few pieces from the shoe with a chisel, weighs them up, and gives small silver or copper coins in exchange, but each time that this happens, unless the merchant watches very carefully, he will find that he has been the loser by a chip or two. The Mexican dollar is now the generally accepted currency, and its value, at par, varies from 1s. 8d. to 2s. Some dollars are stamped with an effigy of the dragon, some with the head of Yuan Shih Kai, and some with the head of Sun Yat Sen. The last are unpopular, and in out-of-the-way places they are rejected on the plea that the " head is too small." This in some way lowers the value of that particular dollar in the eyes of the shop-keepers. The stranger is sure to ask how the money-changer makes a living out of his business as he only gives men change for their coins, and they see to it that he gives them the full amount. Where is the profit? The fact is that exchange varies from town to town, and his business is to buy dollars at a cheap rate and find a means of selling them expensively, sometimes by moving them to another locality, and sometimes by holding them back until the rate of exchange has fluctuated a trifle, and so he manages to work things to his own advantage. It is certain that a money changer's home is never a poor one.

The flags of China always provoke a question. They have changed frequently during the last thirty years, and in the days when she was under Imperial government China's flag had a yellow background with a large dragon across it, symbolic of the glory of the Manchu dynasty and the Emperor who ruled the land. Then came the national flag of the Chinese Republic, with five colours in parallel stripes. The first was red and indicated China proper; below this was a yellow stripe to represent the Manchurian people, black for Tibetans, blue for Mongols and white for Moslems. This five-coloured flag was intended to symbolize the unity of the five racial strains which inhabit China and her dependencies. In 1928 this flag was replaced by the one which is in use everywhere to-day. Its emblem is a white circle set in blue on a red background, and it symbolizes the white sun of equality in the blue sky of liberty on a field of red which stands for brotherhood.

In every town and village there is some building which

bears the inscription *Yu Chen Chü* over the door. The characters mean " Post Office," and although in the cities and large towns the building may be a most imposing edifice, it is the little village shack which is the more interesting. It is here that the real inland courier, riding in from a long journey across mountains, over rivers and deserts, is met. At such a small stage he finds another courier waiting with a fresh horse, and the mail-bags are thrown off one beast on to the other, while the next man leaps to the saddle and carries them as swiftly as possible to the next office. Wherever a man arrives the villagers all gather to hear what news he brings, and to enquire where the letters come from and to whom they are addressed. The envelope is interesting because it carries so much information. On the right hand is first the name of the town, then the street where the house is situated, and lastly the number of the house, for the Chinese argue that it is in this order that an address is traced. In the left-hand corner is the name and address of the sender. If a Chinese is writing to a parent he will consider it a liberty to use his father's name, so he only writes the inscription " To my honourable father." Moreover, there are various instructions on the envelope which urge that it be delivered without delay, such as " Quick as fire! Quick as fire!"

In larger towns a letter-writer can generally be found sitting at a small table outside the Post Office. This man charges a small sum of money for writing a letter, and anyone who is illiterate is glad to employ him. There is always a small crowd listening as he reads the letter aloud to his client, and bystanders comment on the style and the contents, which never fail to excite general interest.

Chinese stamps are a great addition to any collection, for the Chinese like to commemorate national events and to honour patriots by a special issue which celebrates every memorable anniversary.

The postal system of China uses trains, horses, mules, camels or carts for freightage, and now the aeroplane carries most of the first-class mail. The postal organization has always been remarkably good, and the courtesy and kindness of the postmasters is unsurpassed anywhere. Its efficiency is perhaps due to the fact that ever since the thirteenth century China is known to have had a well-organized plan of postal " runners." On every main road there were post-stations where runners were lodged so that letters written by the Ministers of State need never be delayed in transit. These runners wore belts hung over with jingling bells, and they were ready to leave at any hour of the day or night, as required. Specially trained for swiftness, they ran the whole of the three miles to the next post-station, carrying the letters in their girdles. At night the sound of bells roused the next runner from sleep, and he quickly made ready to seize the parcel and speed ahead without a moment's delay. Letters have been carried like this from Canton to Peking. At the present time caravan men, taking long desert stages by night, still hear the jingle of distant bells, and say to each other, " Here comes the letter-carrier." Before long they are overtaken by a courier riding a swift Mongolian pony. With a cheery word of greeting he hurries past to hand over his mail bags to the next man, who stands ready to receive them and take them one stage further.

Every town in China has a *Yamen*, which is equivalent to a Town Hall and is the private residence of the chief City Magistrate, who holds the seal of office. It stands near the centre of the town, and its main entrance shows on to a great open space where much business is transacted. Vendors of all kinds congregate there, and also groups of men discussing impending law-suits, for it is in the outer court that law cases come up for judgment, and in the back premises is the town jail. The official seal is always kept

WATER-TAXIS SPEEDING TOWARDS A LINER ON THE HUANG-PU NEAR
SHANGHAI

[Page 88

HOUSE-BOAT

JUNK

in the *Yamen,* and at nightfall, when the city gates are locked, the great keys are carried there and only fetched away at dawn. On the whitewashed wall facing the main entrance there is a painting of a huge tiger, symbolic guardian of the *Yamen.* The Magistrate is bound to give protection to anyone who is in immediate danger, and at the call " Save life! Save life!" the gates are flung open and the claimant received to safety until his case has been investigated. Many proverbs are in use which show what the Chinese people feel about the *Yamen.* For example, "It is difficult to get inside the *Yamen* door if you have only right but lack money." When a man reaches middle age he is expected to have sense enough to keep free from law cases and, proverbially, he should have left all these follies behind him by the time he is sixty.

In many towns or on hills dominating city walls the visitor will notice high slender towers which have been built in order to dispel evil influences and bring luck to the locality. These towers, he will be told, are called pagodas, and they add greatly to the charm of the landscape because the site on which they are placed has been so well chosen. The pagoda is always built in successive stories, each story having a verandah with a high roof which is pointed at the corners. There may be as few as seven or as many as thirteen, but always an odd number because odd numbers are more lucky than even ones. The commonest shape is the regular octagon, and at each corner there are metal discs which clash as the wind blows and give a resonant sound like bells ringing. The word " pagoda " probably comes from the Persian and means " House of Idols." The highest pagoda in China measures 360 feet, and one of the most beautiful is the Porcelain Tower at Nanking, but the inhabitants of innumerable Chinese cities, looking at their own pagoda, think that it comes nearer to perfection than any other.

There is one common sight in a Chinese town which always intrigues the westerner and makes him say " What is that?" He sees a dignified elderly man wearing a handsome satin coat, and walking down the street with a bird-cage dangling from a short stick of which he holds one end. If questioned he would certainly say that he was taking his bird to a singing lesson. Near by, among the trees of a quiet park, there are other elderly men who have brought their own caged birds, which are all Manchurian larks but which do not all sing equally well. Here by the waterside and among the trees the finest songsters sound their clearest notes, and the others imitate until their own vocal powers are developed and they too can use the whole range of their voice capacity. Away in Mongolia there is a place called the Temple of the Larks, and once a year the bird merchants go there to a great fair in order to buy young larks and carry them away to towns, where rich people will always give a high price for a good songster.

CHAPTER XVII

WHERE IS IT?

CHINESE names are considered difficult to pronounce and hard to remember, but a certain number of them, relating either to personalities or to localities, are so often met with that it is necessary to know them. The following are some of the best known places in China, with sufficient information about them to fix them in the memory. Be sure to have the map at hand when reading this chapter.

Nanking.—This town became the capital of China on June 21st, 1928, by order of the Nationalist Government. The name means Southern Capital, and before the time of the Manchu dynasty it was the chief city of the country. Nanking stands on the right bank of the Yangtse, and is connected by rail with Shanghai. Its principal sights are the Lotus Lake, the Purple Mountain, the Porcelain Tower, and the tomb of Sun Yat Sen, first President of the Chinese Republic. The city wall is thirty-three miles in length, and in the great plan of reconstruction for Nanking one of the chief features is to convert the high encircling wall into a raised motor road which will be one of the panoramic marvels of the world.

Chungking.—It was to this town that the Chinese Government removed on leaving Nanking, and it became the headquarters of the Generalissimo, Chiang Kai Shek. Chungking is on the Upper Yangtse, above the dangerous gorges and at the confluence of the Yangtse and the Kialing Rivers. It is reached by river steamers which are specially constructed for passing over the rapids. Since the fall of Hankow to the Japanese it is generally reached by air or over newly constructed motor roads from the west. It now houses some of China's most famous schools and universities, which were evacuated from northern and eastern centres.

Hankow.—The most important commercial centre of all the Yangtse ports. Connected by rail with Peking and with Canton, and by boat with Shanghai. It is the centre of the tea trade and of the shipping business which conveys inland produce to the coast.

Canton.—The first Chinese town to become an " open port," that is, open to European commerce. The chief exports are silk, tea, matting, sugar, leaf-tobacco and tungsten. It stands to the north of the Sikiang (West River) delta. The ocean-going liners stop at Whampoa, about thirteen miles away.

Hong Kong.—An island and seaport lying off the coast of Kwantung province. It was ceded to Britain by China in 1841 and became a British Crown Colony. The island has a coastline of twenty-seven miles and its hills rise to nineteen hundred feet. Under British control the value of its trade reached about £50,000,000 per annum. The island is noted for its sheltered and beautiful harbour. It was attacked and taken by Japan in 1941 and closed to international trade.

Kunming (or *Yünnanfu*).—An inland town standing on a high fertile plain. It marks the northern extremity of the Burma Road, and on this account has suddenly come into great prominence. The Military School of Aviation is located there.

Foochow.—A seaport at the mouth of the Minkiang (Min River). The ocean liners come no further than Pagoda, which is ten miles away. It is renowned for lacquer-ware and for the manufacture of umbrellas made of varnished paper. The chief exports are sugar, oranges, tea, bamboo and preserved ginger.

Ningpo.—This is a very large town twenty miles from the coast between Foochow and Shanghai. It has given its name to the best varnish of China (sap of the tree Rhus vernicifera), and exports raw cotton, matting and hats.

Changsha.—The provincial capital of Hunan. It is a university town, has important missionary hospitals, and is the centre of export for antimony.

Shanghai.—This great seaport at the mouth of the Yangtse is the fifth largest town in the world. It is in the province of Kiangsu, which has a population of 920 to the square mile, and, for its size, is the most densely populated area in the world.

Sian (or *Changan*).—This town is the provincial capital of Shensi province, and was the capital of China during five dynasties. It was already in existence in 2205 B.C., and is famous for its avenues of inscribed stone tablets, called the

Forest of Pencils, and for the Nestorian tablet dating back tc the seventh century, and inscribed in Chinese and Syriac with the names of many early Chinese Christians.

Peiping (Peking).—During the last ruling dynasty, which was that of the Manchus (1644-1912), this was the capital of China. In 1928 it ceased to be the seat of Republican Government and the residence of the President. It is an inland city, and has world-wide renown for its buildings, temples and art collections. The Peking Union Medical College is the principal centre of medical research in China.

Tientsin.—This is the nearest seaport to Peiping and is situated at the northern extremity of the Grand Canal at the point where it joins the Peiho (North River). It is the largest port of North China, and exports great quantities of coal, wool, furs and cotton.

Urumchi (also called *Tihwa*).—A city which is the capital of Sinkiang. It is situated at the point of extreme distance from any seaport, is surrounded by desert land, and is watered by a river flowing down from the snowfields of the Tien Shan (Heavenly Mountains). It has a cosmopolitan population of Chinese, Russians, Mongolians, Turkis and Tungans, and is a centre of the desert trade-routes which respectively lead to Siberia, across Mongolia, to the Himalayan passes for North India, and to Sian. It also has communication with Lhasa by means of travelling Tibetan lamas. Urumchi will be an important stage on the air route connecting Europe with the Far East, and now has British, American and Russian consulates.

Kashgar.—This town of Sinkiang is situated at the foot of the Himalayas, and is a starting place for travellers over the Karakorum and Gilgit Passes through the Himalayas to North India. There is a British Consul General resident in Kashgar.

Hami (or *Cumul*).—One of the oases of the Gobi Desert which is renowned for its fertility. Its strategic position has made it important as an airport on the Moscow-Shanghai air-line.

Tung-Ting.—This lake lies south of the Yangtse in Hunan. When full it is seventy-five miles long, sixty miles broad, and two hundred and sixty-six miles in circumference.

Po-Yang.—A smaller lake lying between Anhwei and Kiangsu provinces. It is ninety miles long, twenty miles broad, and connects with the Grand Canal.

The Grand Canal.—This artificially made waterway connects Hangchow in the south with Tientsin in the north. Its total length is twelve hundred miles. It dates from 485 B.C.

The Great Wall.—A wall fifteen hundred miles long, leading from Shan-hai-kwan on the Po-hai to Kia-yu-kwan on the north-west frontier of China proper. It dates back to 300 B.C.

The Sacred Mountains of China.—China abounds in Taoist and Buddhist mountain shrines. The following are famous places of pilgrimage which are visited every year by thousands of lamas from Tibet and by pilgrims from many parts of China. Some of the lamas spend years prostrating themselves in the dust of the long roads which connect the mountains.

The most famous is in Shantung and is called the *Tai Mountain* or the Great Eastern Peak. In every city there are lucky key-stones let into buildings which bear the inscription " A stone from the Tai mountain dares to resist " (all evil influences). This is a mountain of remarkable beauty, and at one of the resting-places on the pilgrim's path which leads to the summit is a great slab of stone which was intended as memorial to the Emperor who built the Great Wall. It bears no name and it is said that in resentment of the toll of life and strength which he exacted from his people in carrying through that enormous enterprise, the stone-carvers refused to chisel the inscription which was to commemorate his name.

The second sacred hill is the *Heng Mountain* in Hunan. The eighth month is the special pilgrimage month, and nearly one million people crowd to the large temple at the foot of the mountain in order to worship the idol called Sheng Ti, Holy Emperor. The entire hillside is built over with shrines and temples.

The *Hwa Mountain* or Western Great Peak is in Shensi, not far from Sian. It is a terrible climb to reach the top by the long flights of small steps which lead there, but once the pilgrim reaches the summit a magnificent panorama lies before him.

The *Sung Mountain* in Honan is known as the Middle Great Peak, and is the highest of the sacred mountains. The Chinese have a proverb which says: " A mountain is not judged by its height," and this is true of the Sung Peak, for though the loftiest of the holy hills it is by no means the most popular resort of the pilgrims.

The province of Szechwan has a sacred mountain of special interest. It is called *Mount Omei*, which means the High Eminent Peak, and cutting down one of its sides is the deepest precipice in the world—a fall of six thousand feet. Looking down over its edge pilgrims sometimes see in the abyss below a brilliant disc of light surrounded by a rainbow. This is called " The Glory of the Buddha," and thousands of pilgrims climb the mountain every year in the hope of seeing that sight. Its most treasured relic is a reputed tooth of Buddha, which is twelve inches long and weighs eighteen pounds.

Wutai Mountain in Shansi has a name which means Five Terraces, because of the five risings by which the peak is reached. At one time there were three hundred and sixty monasteries on this mountain, but now they are fewer, although a pilgrimage to Five Terrace Mountain is a privilege coveted by all Buddhists who aim at perfection. Each sacred mountain honours some particular holy being, and the great white pagoda of Wutai holds a special relic, which is one hair from the head of its patron saint.

CHAPTER XVIII

A CHINESE WHO'S WHO

ALL through the ages China has been famous for her great and wise men. Her legendary records go back to remote antiquity, but become historically reliable about 2500 B.C. At that time her emperors already held the title " Son of Heaven," for they were believed to reign by divine appointment and to be vice-regents of *Tien* (heaven). Such a belief laid a heavy burden on the emperor, who became personally responsible for any disaster which might come to his country, and there are wonderful and pathetic passages in Chinese history which tell of emperors accepting responsibility, yet being unable to discover how they had offended against heaven. Therefore, like King David, they pleaded that they personally might be punished and the nation be spared (2 Sam. 24).

There are certain emperors, statesmen, sages, writers, painters and poets who have a place in common talk, and everyone interested in China should know who they are. The Biographical Dictionary of Famous Chinese is an exceedingly large volume, and even this is not complete, so it is obvious that only a very few names can be included in this chapter. But just as any visitor to Britain would be expected to know something of Queen Victoria, Gladstone, Shakespeare, Charles Dickens and Winston Churchill, so the Chinese expect foreigners to know such names as the

CORMORANT-FISHING. EACH BOAT HAS 10 TO 15 BIRDS

HOUSE-BOATS CROWDED IN A SMALL CANAL

Empress Dowager, Sun Yat Sen and Chiang Kai Shek, and to have heard of her philosophers Confucius, Mencius and Laodz.

The earliest known emperor is *Fu-Hsi* (3000 B.C.), who discovered how to tame animals and taught people how to live in families. He evolved a picture writing which they could understand, and when he showed his people how to fish he wrote a song for the fishermen to sing.

The next emperor of note was *Shen Nung*, who taught people how to plough, to sow and to reap, and taught them so well that the Chinese became the best farmers in the world. They learnt from him the great principle that man must not impoverish the earth but should put back as much as he takes from it, so from early times they manured the soil, ploughed in some of their crops, and used the ashes of burnt rubbish as a fertilizer.

Then came *Huang Ti* (The Yellow Emperor) (2700 B.C.). He wore yellow silk robes and his palace was roofed with yellow tiles. The Chinese were then still scattered far and wide, but he gathered them up under one central government. He built boats and carts and made roads, so that transport between various districts became possible. He also instructed his people in the principles of commerce, showing them how to use weights and measures and metal coins. He gathered to his court men who understood astronomy, and with their help he drew up a calendar and showed his people how to use it. His wife, the Empress Lei-tzu, discovered the value of the cocoon spun by a small worm which ate mulberry leaves. By her example and effort sericulture became a main occupation of the women of China.

Between 2350–2250 B.C. two great rulers, *Yao* and *Shuen*, governed the country on the principle that every king is responsible for the conduct of his people. Such monarchs naturally drew great statesmen to them, and the Minister of State, known as the Divine *Yü*, is famous for having mastered the Yellow River in a time of flood. He worked for nine years until by dint of industry he had deepened the channels and raised the dykes. *Yü* is the subject of innumerable legends and folklore tales.

For the next two thousand years a succession of dynasties followed each other, and at the birth of Christ one so famous as to be called the Glorious Han dynasty (206 B.C–A.D 220) was reigning in China. The last emperor but one of the dynasty which preceded the Glorious Han proclaimed himself by the strange title of "*The First Emperor*" (221–209 B.C.). Everything in history was to begin with him, and he attempted to establish his claim by burning all books recording events which happened before his time. Many learned men were horrified at this destructiveness and tried to save libraries of precious documents, but whoever was discovered doing so was executed or exiled for life. Fortunately a few scholars were lucky enough to get their books built up into the hollow section inside the walls of their houses, and when the " First Emperor " was dead and buried, and with him the dynasty collapsed, they brought out the books and started to copy them under the protection of the Glorious Han. This incident of history is always referred to as " The Burning of the Books."

One of the most popular characters of Chinese history is General *Tsao Tsao* (220–155 B.C.). His grandfather was a court eunuch who served under an Emperor of the Han dynasty, and when little Tsao Tsao was a boy he enjoyed sport, especially hawking, and hunted game with a handsome bird on his wrist. Books had but little interest for him and, though at the age of twenty he took a literary degree, he soon found a job more after his own heart as leader of an army which had the declared purpose of setting the Empire to rights and purging the country of all abuses. His discipline was so rigid that no one ventured to disobey him, and one of the most popular stories relates how he was obliged to condemn himself to death because he had un-wittingly allowed his horse to stray in a cornfield. The sentence which he passed on himself would have been carried out but that his friends were so insistent in their demand for a reprieve that at last he reluctantly consented to have his hair cut off instead of his head. Thus both honour and justice were satisfied. Many anecdotes which emphasize his scrupulous sense of honour are told by the market-place story-tellers, as the one which relates how the list of his enemies' names fell by chance into his hands, but he burnt it unread rather than take an unfair advantage of his rival. His chief characteristic was swiftness, decision and quickness of action, and the Chinese proverb which ex-presses speed says: " Call Tsao Tsao and Tsao Tsao is there." He eventually reached a position of such power in the country that his own daughter became Empress.

When his last illness came upon him he sent for a physician, who diagnosed his complaint as " wind under the brain " and assured him it could only be cured by opening the skull and releasing the wind. Old General Tsao Tsao had not lived so long without gaining knowledge of men. He detected a trick to destroy him, sent the doctor to prison and left him there. Before long, however, Tsao Tsao died, but whether the cause of his death was " wind under the brain " has never been confirmed.

Through many centuries China's chief enemies were the roving horsemen who lived a tent life on the grassy plains outside the Great Wall. There were constant clashes on the borders between the armies of the Chinese and the hordes of those Tatar tribes, and sometimes the nomads drove the Chinese back and looted their towns, but next time it might be their turn to be defeated.

In the year 1162 a Mongol boy was born who, under the title of *Genghiz Khan*, was to become one of the most famous men in history. His father was a chieftain, and the family lived in a felt tent. In a few years he was riding about the spaces of Mongolia, and soon became an expert horseman. One day, travelling with his father, they met a man who told them that he had dreamt of a white falcon which, carrying the sun and moon in its talons, perched on his wrist, and he felt convinced that the young man whom he now saw before him was the subject of this dream and would become a great ruler. Being very ambitious, he determined that the boy should marry his own beautiful daughter, so he induced the travellers to accept his hospitality, and the boy was left behind while the father went on his journey.

After some time a messenger rode to the camp, telling of the father's illness and that he wished to see his son before he died. When the boy arrived he found that his father was already dead, and that he himself had now become chieftain of the clan. The men of the tribe refused to follow such a mere boy and all scattered, in spite of the fact that his mother tried to rally them with the symbol of authority in her hand, a standard of nine yak tails.

The young man, however, showed such ability that he soon gathered an army whose soldiers had a great reputation for daring, bravery and cunning. He himself had some amazing escapes from his enemies and won so many followers that he was proclaimed chief of all the Mongols and given the title *Genghiz Khan,* which means " Very Mighty Ruler." Later on, with ten thousand men he went south to fight the Chinese, whom he completely defeated, and returned to Mongolia with an amazing amount of booty. Encouraged by these successes he undertook campaigns in the west, and his hordes pressed forward so rapidly that they reached the banks of the Caspian Sea and came back to their own land laden with more treasures than could possibly be counted. Genghiz Khan was responsible for the death of millions of people. He himself died at the age of sixty-five, and his body was carried back to the land of his birth and buried there under a tree. Later on his grandson, *Kublai Khan,* was not only head of the Mongol Empire but ruler of China also.

The words *" Empress Dowager,"* when used by the Chinese, can only refer to one woman, and that is the great ruler who, at the close of the nineteenth century, shared with Queen Victoria the control of the greater part of the world's inhabitants (1835-1910). The Empress Dowager's official title was "Tzu Hsi," which means "Compassionate and Auspicious," but the People of the Hundred Names have their own opinion of her and always call her " The Old Buddha."

She was a girl of fifteen when the Emperor Tao Kuang died (1850) and his son of nineteen succeeded him. Court mourning was so rigid that he might not marry for twenty-seven months after his father's death, but when this period had elapsed twenty-eight beautiful Manchurian girls were selected for his harem. Among the number was this young Yehonala, who became a lesser concubine of the young Emperor. When she was given this position all intercourse with her own family ceased, but after the birth of her baby boy she was allowed to go home just once and see her parents. As soon as her mother-in-law, consort of Tao Kuang, was dead, Yehonala was promoted to a higher order among the Emperor's concubines, and in due course her own son became heir-apparent to the throne and her position at court was assured. She now began to develop her brilliant powers of intrigue and diplomacy. Her husband, the Emperor Hsien-feng, died young, and when her only son ascended the throne at the age of five she began her first period of regency. He died of smallpox when he was only twenty years old, leaving no child, and the Old Buddha brushed all other claims aside and so handled the Councillors of State that her nephew, then four years old, was proclaimed Emperor, though he was not the heir in direct succession and she was acting contrary to law. Those who opposed her always conveniently died or committed suicide, and Yehonala remained in control of the affairs of state.

When the boy Kuang Hsü came of age she ceased to be Regent but, in fact, she had no intention of lessening her own authority, and by her so-called retirement she attained even higher rank than formerly, for her position as a member of the older generation gave her precedence of the Emperor himself. Some time later it came to her knowledge that he intended to introduce certain measures of reform in the country, and she at once laid her plans to outwit him. The Emperor was acting with a group of friends, and had entrusted one of them, Yüan Shih Kai, with the responsibility of preventing his aunt from again seizing the reins of government. Yüan was false to his Imperial Master, and secretly kept the Old Buddha informed of all that was taking place. One day she suddenly arrived at the Forbidden City from her Summer Palace, which was a few miles from Peking, issued an order that the Emperor be removed to an island on one of the lakes, and she herself assumed the position of supreme authority. A notice was posted throughout the Empire which read: " The Emperor is ill and the Empress Dowager has resumed the regency." Like the Queen in " Alice in Wonderland," she ordered executions right and left, saying: " Trials are unnecessary: let the executions take place immediately!"

At this very time a strange movement was taking place in China which is spoken of to this day as the Boxer Movement, though in Chinese it was called " The Public Spirited Harmonious Band." Its members professed to possess magical powers, the men seized swords and went out to kill, and the women wore red clothes and drilled like soldiers. The Boxer Movement was no doubt aggravated by the westerners' disregard of superstitious fears connected with laying railway tracks through family graveyards and planting telegraph posts on sacred sites, and by newspaper articles discussing the partition of China—all such things helped to create fear, distrust and antagonism. When it was known that the Emperor favoured intercourse with other nations, anti-foreign riots broke out which were encouraged by men in authority. The Governor of Shansi, Yü-hsien, was helping the Empress Dowager, and by her orders fifty-one missionaries with many Chinese Christians were killed in his *yamen* in July, 1900, some of them by his own hand. Prince Tuan, head of the Boxers, was made chief of the Foreign Office. All the western residents in Peking were besieged in the Legation buildings, and the whole of China seethed with unrest. Retribution was inevitable, and a month later the Old Buddha and the Emperor were fleeing before the Allied armies, who were already well on the way to Peking. They escaped to Sian and remained there until negotiations were completed with the offended powers, but when the Court returned from this humiliating flight, the Old Buddha, as usual, played her cards cleverly. She had already murdered the Emperor's wife, " Pearl Concubine," and from this time onwards he himself was a helpless prisoner in her hands. She did all in her power to conciliate the representatives of the foreign nations and invited the ladies of the Embassies to the Palace, received them in her most gracious way, and presented them with white roses as they left. A piece of shattered wall, however, stands to this day by the British Legation in Peking, and on it are written the momentous words: " Lest we forget."

When the Empress knew that she was dying she issued her last orders, and the young Emperor " mounted the phœnix chariot " before she died. Their deaths were announced almost simultaneously.

The overthrow of the Manchu dynasty and the Imperial

rule in China will always be connected with the name of *Sun Yat Sen*, who is frequently referred to as " Father of the Republic." He had spent many years of his life with one object in view—the freeing of China from the yoke of the Manchu Government, which would allow for no progress and which refused to adopt any reforms.

He was born in 1867 in a village near Canton. His father was a Christian, and he was taught English by a woman missionary. He learnt it so well that in 1887 he entered a College in Hong Kong where Chinese students might take a medical course. After his graduation he began to practise in Macao, a Portuguese colony near his own village, where he heard for the first time of the Young China Party, and soon became a very active leader of the revolutionaries. Before long there was a price set on his head and he had many narrow escapes. On one occasion a band of spies came to take him, but he calmly went on reading aloud a volume of classics he held in his hand, and the men became so much interested that instead of arresting him they stayed to discuss the teaching of the book.

The most serious attempt on his life, however, was made in London. He was walking down Devonshire Street on his way to church when a young Chinese spoke to him, and shortly after they were joined by yet another Chinese. These two men invited Dr. Sun to go with them to their lodging, but he refused, saying that he had arranged to meet an English friend, Dr. Cantlie, at church. As they passed near an open doorway the two men forced him into the house, and the door was immediately shut and locked behind them. Sun then realized that he was in the Chinese Embassy and that he was a prisoner. For twelve days he remained locked in a room, during which time he tried by every means to communicate with the outside world. He wrote messages on little pieces of paper and threw them out of the window, hoping that someone would pick them

DINNER IN A CHINESE RESTAURANT

FOOD-VENDOR'S STALL

[Page 104

A CHINESE MERCHANT

NANKING ROAD, SHANGHAI

up and read them, but one note was found by a servant, and the windows of his room were promptly nailed up. Meanwhile plans were on foot to transport him to China as a dangerous lunatic, and he would certainly have lost his life but for the prompt action taken by the English wife of a Chinese Embassy servant. She heard about the mysterious prisoner and wrote a letter to Dr. Cantlie, the missionary who was his friend.

At half-past eleven on the night of October 17th, 1896, there was a ring at Dr. Cantlie's front door, and when he answered it no one was there, but a note had been pushed under the door which read: " A friend of yours is imprisoned in the Chinese Legation here. They intend sending him out to China, where it is certain that they will hang him. It is very sad for the poor man, and unless something is done at once he will be taken away and no one will know about it. I dare not sign my name, but this is the truth, so believe what I say. Whatever you do must be done at once or it will be too late. His name is, I believe, Sin Yin Sen."

Dr. Cantlie went straight to the police station with his report, but no one took the story seriously. " It is a wild tale," they said, " such things do not happen in London." The inspector smiled at Dr. Cantlie's distress and said: " Go home; you have reported the matter to us, and that is enough." The doctor, however, knew that there was a price of £100,000 on Dr. Sun's head, so that his capture was well worth while. Every moment was precious, and seeing that he could not get help from the police, he went straight to the Foreign Office, where a friendly official helped him to take the matter direct to Lord Salisbury.

Embassies are sacred to the land to which they belong, therefore the Chinese Embassy in London was recognized as Chinese soil, and no Britisher, not even the Prime Minister, might enter the premises in order to rescue the

C—4*

standing for suspicion and hostility.

When Japan showed signs of aggression Chiang did not act quickly enough to please the other national leaders, and they accused him of following a policy of appeasement. Chiang, however, knew the uselessness of resistance unless his people would sink their differences and unite to support him. Hearing of trouble in Sian, in the province of Shensi, he flew there to deal with the disaffection, but he was kidnapped by General Chang Hsüeh Liang, son of the celebrated Manchurian war-lord Chang Tso Lin.

The Generalissimo refused to make any concession to his captors or to sign any papers while he was in their hands, and, as head of the state, he absolutely refused to bargain with subordinates. This incident aroused the interest of the whole world, and when Chiang was finally released he was received back in Nanking with such a demonstration of confidence as China has seldom seen. Any doubt regarding his sincerity in the matter of dealings with Japan was silenced, and shortly afterwards, when he summoned the armies to battle, he could be sure of their united support.

Chiang Kai Shek and his wife make no secret of their Christian conviction, and begin each day with Bible reading, meditation and prayer. Visitors to their home are asked to stay to family prayers, and when meeting with Mr. Churchill, President Roosevelt and Marshal Stalin in North Africa the same rule held good, and British newspapers noted that the General and Madame were not accessible to visitors in the early morning as they were engaged in prayer and meditation.

A very difficult pathway lies ahead for the General. As the great war draws to a close there are many parties to be conciliated, and each of them demands some concession. Only that wisdom which is the gift of God can enable him to deal truly and justly with all concerned.

Madame Chiang has gained for herself a unique position

among the notable women of the world. She was born into a very influential family, for her parents, Mr. and Mrs. C. J. Soong, were Christian people with important business interests at Shanghai, and they were enlightened in their views on education and on every other social matter. She was the youngest daughter of a family of six children, and her three brothers, T. V., T. L., and T. A. Soong, are all well-known men. She and her two sisters were called Eling, Chingling and Mayling, and they married respectively Mr. H. H. Kung, Minister of Finance, Sun Yat Sen, Father of the Chinese Republic, and Chiang Kai Shek, Head of the National Government.

Their father himself was educated in America, where he became a Christian, and on returning to China married a girl who had been educated in a Mission School and was a true follower of Christ. She was known to spend long hours in prayer, and was also full of good works. She brought up her own children with spartan severity, and both boys and girls were well educated, first at Mission Schools in China and later in American colleges, for the parents had completely outgrown the idea that the best education was only necessary for boys.

Their father was very friendly with Dr. Sun Yat Sen, with whose political views he was strongly in sympathy. His life was consequently often in danger, and at one time the family was obliged to seek shelter in Japan, as also did Sun Yat Sen and Chiang Kai Shek. Here Eling, the eldest daughter, met Mr. Kung and consented to marry him. Until the time of her marriage she acted as secretary to Dr. Sun, and when the time came to leave him he asked her sister Chingling to take her place. She did so, and before very long she told her parents that she was going to marry him. Her mother most strongly disapproved, and in the end Chingling ran away from home in order to carry out her purpose. She was left a widow in 1925.

General Chiang Kai Shek first met Mayling in Dr. Sun's home, and asked Dr. Sun to help him to win her as his wife. Mrs. Soong would not consent to the marriage and refused even to see Chiang, while on her side Mayling was firm in her determination not to marry without her mother's consent. Chiang waited patiently for five years, at the end of which Mrs. Soong went to Japan to escape him, but he followed her there, and at last she consented to an interview. He told her that he could not promise to become a Christian, but that he could promise to study the Bible. The conversation pleased Mrs. Soong so much that she gave her consent, and the marriage took place on December 1st, 1927. Chiang kept the promise made to his mother-in-law, and later was baptized a Christian.

It is impossible to estimate what the General and Madame have done for China. They have brought a new spirit of unity into a divided and troubled nation. Madame has led the women of China in Red Cross and nursing organizations, and has made herself responsible for some forty thousand war orphans. She herself declares that her most important contribution is helping her husband, and she acts as interpreter during his talks with the British and American Allies. Her knowledge of two hemispheres enables her to interpret the outlook of East to West and of West to East. There is a sense of proportion and balance whenever General and Madame Chiang undertake responsibilities—the balanced judgment which results from the unity of a man's and woman's outlook and gives poise and dignity to their statements.

The occasion on which her tact and insight were in greatest evidence was when her husband was kidnapped in Sian, just before the outbreak of war with Japan. There was a very strong feeling in military circles against the perpetrators of this outrage, and a punitive expedition was organized. It was due to Madame's pleading for patience until full investigation had been made that China was saved from civil war and became united against a common foe. When the leaders on both sides met together and talked reasonably, each saw the best in the other, and came to an agreement by which many lives were spared, bitterness was avoided, and all parties rallied to the help of the General. Madame had many times read those words of Christ: " Blessed are the peacemakers," and she made that blessedness her own.

Feng Yü Hsiang was one of China's war-lords, and is generally known as " The Christian General." He has made a great name for himself in China on account of the patience and thoroughness with which he trained the men of his army both to endure hardness and to uphold a strict standard of conduct. He disciplined his troops with great severity, and yet, as they themselves would say, " he loved us as a father." Many a young soldier fresh from home, and who lay wounded, would find the General sitting by his hospital bedside, making arrangements for his comfort and for messages to be sent to his home. Feng himself lived as simply as his men, and himself obeyed the orders he issued to them—no spirits, no tobacco, no opium. He determined to make his men respected by the populace and valued as protectors of the people's rights. In the early days of his generalship people were afraid of his troops, but they made a good name for themselves wherever they went, for they never took advantage of the common people, and they paid full price, in ready money, for all they bought from the peasants. Any breach of discipline was punished with the utmost severity, and once when his chauffeur knocked over an old man and passed on as if nothing had happened, General Feng got out of the car and shot him dead on the spot. " The people of the hundred names," he said, " must be valued and respected." Feng Yü Hsiang belongs to the Christian Church, and in teaching his men to read he expected them to read the Bible. Whenever he took over the control of a city, one verse from the Bible was written on the walls in huge ideographs: " If any man will not work neither shall he eat."

On many occasions handsome presents were sent to him by Governors and high officials, but they were always promptly returned, and it soon became known throughout every province of North China that the favour of General Feng or his officers could not be bought, and that neither with money nor with honours could he be bribed into any course of action. Like most of the Chinese military leaders, General Feng is now supporting the Generalissimo and the National Government of China against the common enemy. Remember his name, because you may hear of this simple, rugged, uncompromising soldier again in the future.

Yen Hsi Shan is known throughout China as the " Model Governor of Shansi," and he has ruled this most important province since 1911. This in itself constitutes a record. He has concentrated his whole effort on making Shansi a model to all other provinces, and has refused extension of territory and all appointments which would divert energy from that which is his foremost intention. The province is surrounded by mountains, and the railway which enters it cuts right through the hillside and is a marvellous feat of engineering. The line was cleverly built by Belgian engineers, but had to be on such a narrow gauge that no other rolling stock can be used on it. On taking up the Governorship Yen Hsi Shan organized a system of reform which he felt was long overdue. It had three main objectives— schooling for all, unbound feet for women and girls, and a province free of opium—a difficult programme to carry into effect. He opened schools everywhere, for he determined not only to supply higher education to the few, but to teach the masses also, and each midday when the temple bell

KOREAN GENTLEMAN, OR "YANG-BAN." HE IS STRICTLY OPPOSED
TO MANUAL LABOUR AND "HONOURABLE IDLENESS" IS HIS
AMBITION

A CHINESE PIRATE

[Page 112

INTERIOR OF A KOREAN HOME WITH MAN AND HIS WIFE

A PEASANT GIRL

AN OLD MONGOLIAN SHEPHERD

THREE GENERATIONS IN A MANCHURIAN FARMER'S HOME

sounded the adult villagers also gathered for popular instruction. Everyone was expected to learn the simplified writing called the phonetic script, and in the capital of his province he had the basic symbols posted in a prominent place and illuminated at night, so as to be always evident. With opium-smokers he dealt very drastically. They were given a limited time in which to break off the drug habit under free medical care, but if they delayed treatment both men and women were imprisoned, or some were even shot.

The new cities built by Yen Hsi Shan are perhaps the most unusual in China. He calls them "Cities of Overcoming Difficulties." Such towns have been recently hollowed from the mountain-side, and consist entirely of caves which are very cheaply and quickly made, as work can be done in one week, for thirty shillings, which will last for almost a century. In the largest, ten thousand people are already living.

In one "City of Overcoming Difficulties" there are streets upon streets, each section being one story higher than the other. In the caves a daily newspaper is printed, there is a radio station, a theatre, business offices, shops, restaurants, a printing press, a paper factory and other manufacturing plant. One visitor, describing the scene at night-time when the people come out, each carrying a little lighted oil lamp, compares it with the view of Hong Kong harbour when, at sunset, all the lights suddenly show up through the darkness. All this is going on in dwellings which form a perfectly safe shelter from air attacks. Truly, they are well named "Cities of Overcoming Difficulties."

Dr. Hu Shih is a scholar to whom young China owes its emancipation from the bondage of literary tradition. In all matters of literary composition, poetry, philosophy, in the realm of religion and in the field of education, there has been an immemorial and binding custom that all Chinese writing must be in the *wenli* or literary script. This is not a spoken language, and a great deal of the scholar's life was spent in acquiring *wenli* and in learning to express himself by its means. It is strictly a literary form and used by scholars exclusively for scholars.

Dr. Hu Shih, a man of renowned learning, a graduate of Cornell and Columbia Universities, Professor of Philosophy and Chairman of the Department of English literature in his own university, saw that the future of Chinese education lay in the amalgamation of Western and Eastern cultures, and that this union was incompatible with stereotyped Chinese literary tradition. He realized that the way to gain the best from each must involve a " literary revolution," the outcome of which would be freedom to use ordinary Chinese language in writing as well as in speech. On the first day of January, 1917, Dr. Hu Shih launched this great campaign and its success was amazing, for within four years he and his co-workers had exercised such a powerful influence on national thought that the Ministry of Education issued a decree ordering that all text-books in lower grade schools should be written in the vernacular. The benefits were so quickly apparent that the order was soon extended to higher grade departments, and the government followed up the new scheme with the publication of a vernacular dictionary. Very soon treatises on the most profound subjects were being written in simplified style and works of all kinds were being translated from foreign languages into colloquial Chinese.

Simplified writing has brought the literature of all other lands within the reach of the Chinese reading public, and the publishing and book-selling business has become a great feature of both town and country life. It is interesting to observe that in this field also the Christian missionary has done the pioneer work, for the Scriptures were translated into Mandarin, which is the spoken language of the greater part of China, in the very early days of missionary enterprise.

War conditions have rallied many men of great ability to national service in China. The size of this volume will not allow for an adequate list and it is impossible at present to say which of them will prove to be final bene-factors of the nation. Those of whom mention has been made are pioneers in the field of reform, and have left an indelible impression on some side of the life of China's people. Outside China are the remarkable men she has sent as ambassadors to other lands, and her representatives in England alone include such names as Dr. Alfred Sze and Dr. Wellington Koo. As the story of her resistance to aggression becomes clearer the outstanding personalities who have led her various political parties in the way of national progress, as well as those who have been her quislings, will appear more clearly.

CHAPTER XIX

CHINESE ART AND POETRY

FROM the Chinese point of view every painter is a poet, and every poet must have the eye of a painter, because no artist from that land would sit down with paints and a brush merely to reproduce the scene which lay before him. " The artist," it is said, " must first chasten his heart and broaden his spirit by contemplation." Before he can hope to reproduce flowers, streams or mountains, he must live with the scene and absorb impressions of the line, the form and the changing colours of his subject. No one, they say, can paint a tree until he has noted how it looks in the morning light, under the midday sun, or in the evening shadows, and how it varies in changing seasons, under bright skies and under dull skies. The true artist must look into the meaning of it all, and then express it with a few strokes of the brush or a few lines of poetry.

Where the western artist paints portraits of noted men and beautiful women, the Chinese painter is expected to convey the same quality of charm by means of the swaying lines of a bamboo grove, and to suggest the aloofness of exceptional intelligence in the sternness and severity of a single tree.

The question of perspective in Chinese art is often puzzling to the westerner, and it is important to remember that all Chinese landscapes are supposed to be painted from the summit of a high mountain. The ruling principle of the artist's work is always to leave something to the imagination. The Chinese people express their artistic sense through everything which they touch, and their buildings, be they large or small, have curved roofs which merge into the landscape and are never obtrusive. " The Chinese roof implies peace, and bows modestly before the firmament, as is fitting in the place where we humans dwell." The form of pavilions and the outline of camel-back bridges and pagodas have the same central idea—to be part of the landscape and to add beauty to the scene.

The greatest of all Chinese painters is acknowledged to be *Wu Tao Tse*, who lived in the eighth century A.D. He painted animals with such understanding of their character that his admirers made up a whole folk-lore about pictures which came to life. One donkey which he painted on a monastery wall was criticized by the monks, so during the night it walked off the wall and kicked their furniture to bits—or so runs the tale. Once when sitting by a pond and painting a fish the wind caught the paper and blew it to the water-side. When the artist rescued it the paper was quite blank, because the painted fish had swum away downstream. It is related that his pictures of the Buddhist hell were so frightening that people trembled when they saw them, and many gave up their evil ways.

In the British Museum there are pictures by many great Chinese artists, and those who look at them carefully will find them so attractive that they feel they would like to join the happy family parties strolling in the gardens, feast with them in the pavilions, or saunter among the flower-beds and chase the birds flitting to and fro through the moon-gates.

There are many good translations of Chinese poetry, and to read such a poem as the one written below is surely to see and to feel all that is described so cleverly in such a few words.

Thoughts of Home on a Spring Day

The almond trees are nodding, nodding,
    Where sweet waters flow;
Green willows in the breeze are swaying,
    Swaying to and fro.

The girls are gaily singing, singing,
    Songs of long ago,
As they go water-chestnut picking,
    On the lake below.

The merry crowds are laughing, laughing,
    Jesting as they row.
But my own thoughts are homeward turning.
    Would that I could go!

Meng Yün Ching.

THE POEM OF " TEN ONES "

A flower,
A willow,
A fisherman
On a rock.

A ray of sun
On the river,
A bird on the wing.

Half way
Up the mountain
A priest slowly climbs
To a half-ruined shrine.

In the forest
A yellow leaf
Flutters and falls.

Ho Pei Yü.

Translated from the Chinese by Henry H. Hart, A.B., J.D., R.A.S.

CHAPTER XX

TWO CHINESE STORIES

THE people of China love to hear a good story, and there is no more popular person in the market-place than the professional story-teller, who relates incidents connected with national heroes, tells of the wit and resource of outstanding men, and delights his hearers by dramatic recitals of popular legends.   There is always a crowd around him, and when he collects the cash everyone is generous, for they all enjoyed his performance. The following stories are well known and very popular:

JUDGE PAO CHENG DECIDES A HARD CASE

At the time when the Sung dynasty reigned in China there was a Mandarin named Pao Cheng who was renowned for the wisdom of his judgments. He never took a bribe and never allowed his decisions to be influenced by the social standing or the wealth of a claimant, but always stood for the right, and everyone recognized his discernment in detecting the guilty party. He was kind to the unfortunate and all the people loved him, so that they made up a saying about him which ran like this:

" In the heavens there are gods;
    On the earth is Judge Pao Cheng."

He travelled over a long circuit in which he administered justice, and one day from his sedan-chair he saw a small village boy holding an empty basket and sobbing bitterly. The Judge ordered his chair-bearers to stand and he called the boy to his side. " What are you crying about?" he asked.

" I am a seller of fried dough-cakes, Lao -ye,"* said the boy.

" That's nothing to cry about," said the Judge.

" I have lost all my day's takings," wept the boy.

" How much?" asked Pao Cheng.

" Two hundred cash " was the answer.

" How did you lose them?"

" They were taken from my basket while I slept."

" Where had you put down the basket?"

" On that flat stone," said the child.

" If you put it on the stone, then the stone must have

*Lao -ye: a term of respect.

taken the money," said the Judge solemnly. The boy stared while the men in the crowd began to titter. Taking no notice at all of this, Pao Cheng issued an order: " Take the accused stone to the *yamen* and the case will proceed." Four strong men slung the stone to bamboo poles and carried it to the Mandarin's residence while the villagers crowded to hear the case. When Pao Cheng appeared the court was thronged. He took his seat and ordered the stone to be brought.

" Stone," he said very severely, " did you steal the boy's money?"

The stone remained silent, so he ordered it to be lashed with canes. All the villagers began to laugh at this far-cical law case. Then Judge Pao Cheng looked round very angrily, and beating his table with a flat stick he said:

" This laughing is an insult to the court, and everyone present is under punishment of three days' imprisonment."

The people became very frightened, because it was a busy season in the farming world, and to be kept from field work for three whole days was a serious business. They begged forgiveness, promising never to offend again, and the elders of the village kowtowed and undertook to stand surety for the remainder. Pao Cheng then relaxed his severity, and said that instead of imprisonment he would fine them twenty cash each and let them go home. " Bring a butt of water," he said to his attendants, " and let each man throw twenty cash in it."

The crowd was delighted to get off so easily, and the first two who threw in their cash went off happily. When it came to the third, Pao Cheng, who was watching carefully, saw a little oil floating on the surface of the water. " Search that man," he ordered. It was done, and one hundred and eighty oily cash were found on him.

" Let all the rest go free," said the Judge, " but take the

GROUP OF TIBETANS

A YOUNG MANCHU WOMAN

Page 120]

MONGOLIAN WOMAN WITH HER CHILD RIDING THE FAMILY OX

A FIVE-ARCHED "PAI-LOU" GUARDING ENTRANCE TO THE MING TOMBS

two hundred cash and give them back to the boy, then let the thief have a thrashing.''

The villagers went out amazed at the Magistrate's cleverness, and repeating to one another:

> '' In the heavens there are gods;
> On the earth is Judge Pao Cheng.''

THE MOTHER OF MENCIUS

There is one woman whom Chinese historians have exalted as the embodiment of all the virtues. She was the mother of the great sage Mencius, who was born in 372 B.C. In a small book called the '' Three Character Classic,'' which is used by all Chinese school children, there are a few sentences which suggest the particular quality of her greatness. When the ideographs are explained to the child, he is told the following story:

When the philosopher Mencius was a child, his mother sent him to a school where he was to learn all that the boys of that period were expected to know. After a few days he was tired of repeating aloud the long passages which he was expected to memorize, and still more tired of the beatings which he received when he failed to repeat correctly all that his schoolmaster had given him to learn. So he left school and ran home.

His mother questioned him as to why he was back so early, and he told her that he was tired of learning and wanted to play. At that very moment she was weaving cloth at her loom, and a most beautiful pattern was growing under her skilful hands. Without a word she seized her large scissors and cut the warp, leaving her work ruined. Little Mencius called out in horror and distress:

'' What have you done, my Mother? Your lovely pattern is spoilt!''

'' I have done exactly what you are doing, my son,'' she replied. '' You began to study, and that is like the weaving of a beautiful pattern, but you tired of the work and thoughtlessly broke away from it. You can see by what I have done how serious your action is."

This incident made a deep impression on Mencius, and he at once went back to the school.

His mother, however, watched him closely, and she noticed that, when joining with other children in their games, he always copied what he saw going on around, and even led them to play at chasing and killing in the manner of a butcher who lived near. Seeing this his mother moved her home to a more desirable place, but here she found that the children were staging funerals and imitating a group of professional wailers who lived near by. This also displeased her, so she moved again, and this time she decided to make her home next door to a good school. From now on, little Mencius followed the example which was always before his eyes, and became a studious boy. He grew up to be a renowned philosopher and the counsellor of kings.

CHAPTER XXI

THE RELIGIONS OF CHINA

THE Chinese are convinced that religion is essential to every human being, and that any man who professes to have none should be ranked as a barbarian. They are, however, very tolerant as to what form that religion may take, and no one is likely to suffer acute persecution on account of his faith. " Good words should be listened to with respect from whatever source they come," is a saying which sums up the mental attitude of the Chinese people on the subject of a man's creed.

Confucianism, Taoism and Buddhism, because of their widespread influence on the life of the nation, are regarded as " the three religions of China." The first two originated in China and the third in India. These three religions have now so merged into one stream that they cannot well be separated. The same household will reverence the ancestral tablets according to the teaching of Confucius, burn incense before the shrine of Buddha, and call in the Taoist priest to fix an auspicious date for an impending marriage or funeral. Speaking generally, Confucianism has influenced the intellectual side of Chinese life, Buddhism its philosophical side, and Taoism its mystical side. " Confucianism is the most honoured, Buddhism the most loved, and Taoism the most feared."

Confucius (551-479 B.C.) was a very wise teacher and statesman. He believed and taught that sincerity in human relationships constitutes the basis of social and family goodwill, and also that the living members of each family are bound up with the spirits of their ancestors. Therefore one room of each house must be set apart to hold the tablets which record the names of those who have gone before, and here the living burn incense and bring offerings at stated times. This is the basic Confucian teaching of ancestor worship. Each year at the spring festival, family graves are tended and repaired, while paper flowers, paper money, paper clothes and anything which might be acceptable to the departed is piled up and burnt while near relatives wail for the dead. By these means the living are constantly brought into touch with those who have passed on. They are never absent from the thoughts of the younger generation, and their presence is recognized on all such occasions as births, deaths and marriages, where family life is affected.

The four sacred books which the Confucianist must study, and which have been the basis of Chinese scholarship, are:

" The Analects ";
" The Great Learning ";
" The Doctrine of the Mean (or Middle Way) ";
" The Writings of Mencius."

These books contain the sayings of Confucius and of Mencius, collected by their disciples, and among them are many true and wise axioms, such as: " Never do unto others what you do not like done to yourself "; " Do not be distressed because men do not understand you, but rather because you do not understand men "; " Sincerity is the end and beginning of things; without sincerity there would be nothing. Therefore the superior man regards the attainment of sincerity as most excellent."

The outlook of scholarly Chinese is profoundly influenced by Confucian teaching, as the following quotation shows: " An educated man should, above all, be a reasonable being who is always characterized by his common sense, his love of moderation and his restraint." Lack of adaptability to the need of the hour or inability to be reasonable are conditions of mind which are severely condemned by " The Doctrine of the Mean."

Laodz (604-500 B.C.), on whose teaching Taoism is founded, was an older man than Confucius but contemporary with him. He was a great thinker, and he came to certain philosophical conclusions which he expressed in what he called the " *Tao*." This is a word which means " road," " way," or " path," and he explained that this Tao is the *way* that every man should try to find and to follow. " There is nothing," he said, " which the Tao cannot accomplish." The Taoist books include " The Book of Rewards and Punishment," which also has many wise sayings: " Do not publish the faults of others, nor praise your own goodness "; " First correct yourself, then set about correcting others."

Many followers of Laodz, instead of submitting to the

stern discipline which his teaching advocated, began to practise different kinds of magic, and to-day the Taoist priest is called in to choose lucky days on which it would be safe to change a residence, to begin building a house or to start on a journey. He sells charms, practises astrology, and encourages the superstitious fear of demons, which is so strong among simple people, but he finds his most profitable business in connection with what is known in China as *feng shui* (wind and water). This is the art of choosing a site on which to build a house, to dig a grave, or to erect a pagoda so as to bring luck to the neighbourhood and to avoid disturbing the forces of wind and water. The Taoist priest tells fortunes, and declares himself able to counteract all evil influences by means of charms and by chanting incantations.

Buddhism is generally believed to have reached China about A.D. 67 with the coming of two Buddhist priests from India. The Buddha himself was born in the sixth century B.C. in a small village near Benares. He belonged to a noble family, was very wealthy, and had a beautiful wife and child, but he could not find happiness, for nothing satisfied him, and as the days went by his distress increased so much that in the end he abandoned rank, riches and home, and went out to try and find the solution to his problems.

One day when sitting under a tree he had a vision in which he received a revelation of the truth concerning life. He meditated on this for a whole day and night, and then told his companions what he had discovered. They were so deeply impressed that they gave him the name of Buddha —one who is more than human. This claim, however, Buddha never once made for himself, and though his disciples regarded him as a god he made no claims to the state of deity. His teaching was pure, and required of his followers that they should observe rightness of speech, of action, of living and of thinking, that they should devote themselves largely to meditation, and he enjoined five commands, apart from which he had no book of laws. The commands were:

Thou shalt not destroy life;
Thou shalt not steal;
Thou shalt not lie;
Thou shalt not drink intoxicants;
Thou shalt not live impurely.

Buddhist teaching was gradually mixed with much superstition and overlaid with tradition. In its purest form it is not idolatrous, but Buddhist temples in China hold many painted and carved figures before which the worshippers prostrate themselves. Sometimes there is a dark gallery hollowed from the cliff in which the scenes from the Courts of Hell are portrayed. They represent with repulsive realism the tortures to which men who gave way to sin in this life will be subjected after death.

The state religion of both Tibet and Mongolia is Buddhism, and in both these countries it has taken a form known as Lamaism, from the name lama, which is used for the Tibetan Buddhist monk. One child from each home is given to the temple and becomes a lama, and the government of Tibet is vested in two men, the Dalai Lama, who is spiritual head, and the Panchan Lama, who is political head of the country. In the great lamaseries hundreds of lamas live together and spend their time in reciting endless liturgies.

Apart from the " three religions of China " there is Mohammedanism, which, nevertheless, is the creed of many millions of Chinese subjects. For political reasons it is given official recognition by the government, and Moslem Chinese were represented by the white stripe in the five-coloured flag of China. This religion is called Mohammedanism, the Moslem creed, or Islam, which is the name used by Mohammed himself, who was its founder (about A.D. 567-632). His father died shortly before he was born, and he was brought up by relatives. When he was still a youth he went to the Arabian desert and lived for a time among the nomad Bedouin tribes, but later on he took to a business life. After a time he professed to be receiving divine revelations, which appointed him to be the mouthpiece of Allah to men. At first he only told his own relatives, and when the news spread his followers still formed a secret society, the centre of which consisted of members of his own family. When his pretensions became known they raised considerable antagonism, and his life would have been in danger but for the fact that the town of Mecca, in which he sheltered, was a city of refuge in which no blood might be shed. The authorities finally got over this difficulty and went to his house to slay him, but he had been warned and he escaped, leaving his cousin Ali in his own bed to die in his place. This flight of Mohammed turned out to be the turning-point in his career, and from that time the success of his mission was assured. Mohammedanism spread rapidly, and its " prophet " became the dictator of a constantly increasing multitude of followers. His teaching centres on the declaration that there is but one God, and the Moslem profession of faith is: " Allah is one, and Mohammed is his prophet."

The ambition of every Moslem is to make a pilgrimage to Mecca. When he has done this he receives special respect from his fellow-religionists and is honoured with the title of Hadji. Friday is the day observed for worship, and wherever a Moslem prostrates himself in prayer, he turns his face towards Mecca, which was the birthplace of Mohammed.

Moslems practise some rigid forms of religious discipline. Five times each day they recite a prayer. The drinking of intoxicants is not allowed. Eating pork or any product of the pig is absolutely forbidden. For one month of each year there is a rigid fast, when no one may touch food or drink between sunrise and sunset. Women must go veiled outside their own homes. The strict observance of this code of conduct which is required of Moslems links them into one brotherhood all over the face of the earth. Their building for religious gatherings is called a mosque. It has a high tower called a minaret, from which the call to prayer goes forth five times a day.

The first embassy from Arabia to the Court of China was in A.D. 651, but the coming of the Islamic religion was by the overland route across Central Asia, by the trade-routes of the Gobi Desert. Mohammedanism is the religion of the people of Sinkiang, and there are large colonies of Moslems in the province of Kansu. They have caused trouble by their frequent rebellions, the object of which has been to upset Chinese government and establish their own rule. They have, however, never been finally successful in bringing this about.

CHAPTER XXII

CHINA AT WAR

China, the land of culture, of aloofness, of carefully guarded tradition and of proud self-sufficiency, was finally forced into intercourse with other nations, and in so doing inevitably became involved in world problems which were not of her own making. It was the strength of Britain's maritime commerce which by the middle of the nineteenth century first compelled her to open her ports to international trade, and before the close of the nineteenth century she was at war with Japan, and this left her impoverished and robbed of some of her important territory. Twenty years later her age-long system of Imperial government collapsed, and

THE TOMB OF SUN YAT SEN

VICTORIA PEAK, HONG KONG

[Page 128

LIFE IN PATTINGER STREET, HONG KONG

she emerged from the Revolution as a republican country full of new thought and new vision. Unfortunately from that moment China became the prey of contending war-lords, each of whom was out for the satisfaction of his own private ambition. Under their tyranny the " Hundred Names People " were plundered, ill-treated, and suffered loss in life and property.

During the European war (1914-1918) Chinese coolies were recruited and shipped to France, where they served in the Labour Corps on the battlefield. What they saw there must have influenced them toward the belief that inter-national difficulties could not be settled by the " reasonable-ness " which Confucian teaching extols, but only by the power of armed attack and resistance. At the same time the people of Sinkiang were seeing a new aspect of western life when White Russian refugees begged their bread in the *bazars* of oases towns and young Russian women were glad to accept the protection of Chinese men by becoming their secondary wives. Meanwhile one aggressor was casting such greedy eyes on China's eastern provinces that the people learned to fear her as they feared no other nation. For many years it had been evident that Japan coveted Shantung, one of China's most valued provinces, as a sphere of influence. After the European war the valuable port of Kiaochow in Shantung was taken from the Germans, who held it as compensation for the massacre of two nationals, and handed over to Japan. The people of China feared and said: " Whoever holds Shantung grips China like a man grips the throat of his victim." They feared, but could offer no resistance, and gradually Japan extended control over the railway in Shantung, enforced Japanese currency, and even compelled the people to use Japanese stamps on their letters. Penetration was active, and those who knew most feared most.

Japan had long held a treaty by which she was empowered to station her troops in Southern Manchuria, but in 1931 she cunningly tested her power by staging a couple of incidents which would show how far she might go without incurring the censure of the League of Nations. One of these was an explosion on the Manchurian railway line on September 18th, 1931, followed by seizure of Moukden, capital of Manchuria. This worked so successfully that in a few days all the larger cities of Southern Manchuria were in Japanese hands. When the Nanking government considered the matter it issued orders that the incident would be referred to the League of Nations in accordance with the decisions taken in Geneva, and that the army should not resist. The League, however, took no action, and within three months Japan was in control of the three provinces which we call by the general name of Manchuria or Manchukuo. Japan's plan was to gain control over North China, to hold the rich coalfields of Shansi, to impede China's intercourse with the U.S.S.R., and so to terrorize the Chinese Government and people that when they moved forward there would be no resistance to their attack. Under the pretext of manœuvres her armies edged closer to Peiping, and the Chinese even witnessed the sight of Japanese soldiers in gas-masks driving tanks through their streets. The populace had never seen such a horrible sight nor heard so terrifying a noise, yet there was no demonstration and no abuse, only sullen anger and a determination that such aggressive actions should not be allowed to continue.

On July 7th, 1937, the double-seventh as the Chinese call it, the Japanese, on the pretext that one of their soldiers was missing, demanded entrance to the town of Wanping. This was refused and fighting began. By August 13th Peiping and Tientsin had fallen and fighting had reached Shanghai. China, although utterly unprepared for a major war, rose to the occasion, and Shanghai, which the Japanese reckoned to overrun in a few days, held out for two months, meeting mechanized warfare with her bare hands. The whole story of suffering and courage has yet to be told. The well-armed and well-equipped Japanese forces successively captured Peiping, Tientsin, Shanghai, Nanking and Hankow. They moved north, took Taiyuan and spread over Shansi. They landed in southern waters and seized Canton and later Hong Kong.

The Chinese Government moved west to Chungking, and all the political parties, realizing the imminent danger, resolved to stand united with the Government for the purpose of defeating the common enemy. Homeless millions abandoned towns, villages and farms and trekked west. Farmers, formerly very provincial in outlook, were now brought into contact with fellow countrymen of whom they had previously thought as strangers and almost outsiders. Transport had always been difficult, and the ordinary tradesman or farmer until then had lived in his own town or village and seldom moved from it. Now he actually found himself in strange places which had formerly been mere names to him, and he was forced to mix with fellow countrymen who spoke strange dialects and whose homes were among the rice-fields of the south, while his life had been spent among the wheat-fields of the north. Here were men whose outlook on life, though basically Chinese, differed as widely from their own as that of a member of the Italian nation might differ from a Britisher.

This compulsory intermingling of the Chinese people has been exceedingly good for all concerned, and has helped to bring home to all a sense of the vastness of their own land. Students and schoolboys tramped a thousand miles to find a place where they might study in peace, and schools and universities which had been *blitzed* in northern cities were reopened in all kinds of strange premises in the far west. Caves among the mountains were used as laboratories, huts erected by the boys themselves were their class-rooms, and where there was no possibility of premises they studied in the open air. Their determination was that the Japanese should not succeed in destroying the education and culture of China. They might destroy the buildings, but so long as teachers and scholars held together the vital part of school life remained.

Women, in accepting and bearing heavy responsibility, have justified the outlook of New China, which believes in the equal capacity for service of both sexes. A report of the Chinese Ministry of Information contains the following words: " No society ever remains static, especially one which is at war. In China, dynamic forces were released by the major hostilities, and many evacuations have now been in progress over a period of years. Though points of detail are still blurred by the battle-smoke hanging low over charred fields and ruined cities, yet occasional breezes lift the screen to reveal the general outline of a new nation, a new spirit, and a new outlook on life."

CHAPTER XXIII

THE COMING OF CHRISTIANITY TO CHINA

PART I

UNRECORDED history can only claim a place in the field of traditional or legendary lore, but, on the basis that mission-ary effort was the main activity of the Christian community in its earliest times, it seems more than probable that the complete silence regarding so many of Christ's disciples can be accounted for by the fact that they were scattered abroad over the trade-routes of the world, carrying the news of the Gospel to all peoples. About A.D. 140 Justin Martyr made the following declaration: "There exists not a people, whether Greek, barbarian or any other race, by whatsoever title or manners they may be marked out, however ignorant of art or of agriculture, whether they dwell under tents or wander in covered waggons, among whom prayers are not offered in the name of a crucified Jesus to a Father of all."

In the first century of the Christian era, the country we call China had considerable commercial contact with Rome. The woven silk materials produced in Cathay were conveyed to Bactria over the camel routes which crossed the Desert of Lob, where merchants of the Mediterranean lands met the caravan leaders and transacted business with them. In fact, the main trade-road over the desert and the Pamirs was spoken of as the "Silk Road," and the far-eastern country famous as the native region of the silkworm was called by the Romans "Land of the Seres." Tradition, handed down through the centuries, claims that St. Thomas, after founding Christian colonies in Southern India (circa A.D. 52), followed this overland road into Kashgaria, and was first to preach the Gospel among the oases of Central Asian deserts. The truth of this tradition cannot be established, though it is not an improbable story, but the Central Asian plateau was unquestionably one of the main areas in which early Christianity exercised its missionary zeal.

By A.D. 150 the Church was firmly settled in Northern Mesopotamia, and from there Christianity was being propagated through Persia to Bactria. In the early days of Constantine (A.D. 311) Christian missionaries went forth to such distant lands as Scythia and the Crimea, and it is not difficult to think that some of them followed the line of trade-roads which had been used by Alexander the Great and his conquering armies, and which led to the Tarim Basin. Arnobius refers, though vaguely, to Christianity as having been preached among the Seres (or Chinese) before the conversion of Constantine.

The next epoch-making date is A.D. 635, for this was the year in which a Christian Bishop made a perilous journey from Persia, following the course of the Oxus, over the heights of the Pamirs down to the desert plain, in order to bring the knowledge of Christianity to the old civilization of the Chinese Empire. This date is doubly significant because in that same year 635 St. Aidan set out from Iona to convert the pagans of Northumbria to Christ. Thus, at the same moment, Christian missionaries reached the small and backward Kingdom of Northumbria and the vast and highly civilized Empire of Cathay.

The Bishop from Persia belonged to the Nestorian Church, which on account of its resistance to the authority of Rome has been called the " Protestantism of the East," and because of its missionary zeal is often spoken of as "The Church on Fire." The Nestorian Church was called by the name of its leader Nestorius, who was native of a city in Northern Syria called Germanicia. In A.D. 428 he was appointed Patriarch of Constantinople, but later was excommunicated by the Roman, or Western, section of the Church. He found two theological parties in Constantinople, which were bitterly opposed to each other. One of them called the Virgin Mary *Theotokos*—Mother of God while the other called her " the Mother of Man." The members of one sect were called Monophysites * and those of the other Dyophysites. † Nestorius belonged to the latter school, and he proposed that her title should more rightly be " Mother of Christ "—in Syriac "Mother of Messiah."

---

*Monophysite : One of a sect, in the ancient Church, who maintained that the human and divine natures in Jesus Christ became so blended and confounded as to constitute but one nature.

†Dyophysite : A holder of the doctrine of the co-existence of two natures, the divine and the human, in Christ.

From the use of these terms there arose one of the most far-reaching controversies in the history of the Church, so that a council was summoned in 431 to meet at Ephesus, which culminated in a solemn conclave of one hundred and ninety-eight bishops, who unanimously condemned Nestorius as a heretic and decreed that he should be excommunicated from all sacerdotal fellowship. Finally he was banished from his convent in Antioch, whence he went to Arabia and then to Egypt. He is believed to have lived until the year 439 and to have died in Egypt.

The section of the Church which was called by his name obeyed above all others the missionary command to carry the Gospel to all nations, and the golden age of Nestorian missions in Central Asia extended from the end of the fourth century to the close of the ninth. It was through this medium that, for the second time, Christianity came to the people of China.

The methods of Nestorian missionaries seem unusual to men of our time. They went as representatives of no organization or society, but either as craftsmen such as carpenters, smiths or weavers, starting industries in the land of their adoption, or as scribes and secretaries to wealthy employers. " At home they were denounced as heretics, abroad where no rumours of miserable doctrinal disputes were heard they simply journeyed as enthusiastic missionaries of the Gospel." There is no exact information as to when a Nestorian Metropolitan was first appointed to China, but the Patriarch Timothy, writing about the year 790, mentions that the Metropolitan of China had just died.

East and West Turkestan, Mongolia and Southern Siberia, all came under the influence of the Nestorian missionaries, and the honour of having carried the Gospel of Jesus Christ to the Turco-Tatar tribes of Central and Eastern Asia is due to the "untiring zeal and marvellous spiritual activities of the Nestorian Church "—the most missionary Church the world has yet seen.

The influence of Christianity permeated from the extreme north-western provinces towards Central China. In Sian (also called Chang-an), capital of Shensi province, there stands to this day a site of great interest to scholars. It is called " The Forest of Pencils," and there the Chinese keep their most precious stone monuments, including the Confucian writings chiselled on huge blocks of stone. The most important and interesting tablet of the collection is known all over the world as the Nestorian Monument.* Just over nine feet high, three and a half feet wide and one foot thick, the huge slab was hewn from the renowned stone quarries of Fu-ping-hsien. In the centre of the figure-head is the apex of a triangle forming a canopy with nine carved Chinese characters, the literal meaning of which is " Monument commemorating the propagation of the Luminous Religion in the Middle Kingdom." Above these is a Cross which bursts into flowers at each point, and which, strange to say, resembles the Cross on St. Thomas's tomb in South India. Below is a long inscription consisting of one thousand nine hundred Chinese characters and of fifty Syriac words, besides seventy Syriac names transliterated into corresponding Chinese characters. The symbol of the Cross is proof sufficient that the stone is a Christian monument. The slab is clearly dated, and was completed, or, more correctly, unveiled, on the 4th February, A.D 781. The Chinese inscription states this quite clearly: " Erected in the second year of the Chien-chung period (781) of the Great Tang (Dynasty), the year-star being Tso-o on the seventh day of the first month, the day being the great Yao-sen-wen." And again: " In the year one thousand and ninety-two of the Greeks (1092 − 311 = 781) was erected this stone tablet."

*" The Nestorian Monument in China." P. Y. Sheki. S.P.C.K.

COOLIE ON THE HARBOUR FRONT, HONG KONG

THE EMPRESS DOWAGER

PORTRAIT OF CONFUCIUS

Lower down is a long list of names, written both in Syriac and in Chinese. They include " My Lord John, Bishop; Isaac, Joel, Michael, Mahadad Goushnasaf, priests; Bachus and Elias, monks; John, minister and secretary," etc., etc. This splendidly preserved stone tablet, which is as old as Charlemagne, establishes in a detailed manner the position held in China by the Christian Church which is called Nestorian.

After the close of the ninth century Nestorianism gradually declined, the Christian witness lost its clear note, and finally became indistinguishable from the other religions of the land.

It may well be asked why this great missionary movement left so little in the way of a visible Church among the people where it once had such influence. There are many reasons for its decadence, and these should be studied carefully by the missionary student of the present day, for there are important lessons to be learned from it.

With the spread of Islam a great persecution spread over the lands where Nestorians* had preached Christianity, for as the Moslems spread their faith they destroyed with bigoted zeal all those who differed from them. The religion of Central Asia to this day is largely that of Islam. Persecution, however, is never the final factor in the destruction of a Christian Church. Far otherwise, it results in a smaller yet stronger and purer body of men and women who are ready, if needs be, to die for the faith. The more subtle danger is that of compromise and, in time, " the Buddhism of China borrowed largely from Christian doctrine minus the Christian doctrine of the atonement in any reference to a Saviour who died for men and was delivered for their offences."

Buddhism took much that was important from Christianity, but compromised its message to suit the religion of

*" Nestorian Missionary Enterprise," by Rev. J. Stewart, M.A., Ph.D.

Buddha. There was a levelling up on the one hand and a toning down on the other—the spirit of compromise was abroad, and it was a question of give and take. There seems to have been no denial of fundamental doctrines, but just a decline in the note of urgency and definiteness, so that when the awful storm burst the converts were able the more easily to slip into some other expression of what, after all, appeared not too much unlike Christianity, never perceiving that without Jesus Christ as the only Saviour of mankind, and His Cross, atonement and resurrection as the core of their belief, they were no longer Christians.

There was, however, one other fundamental reason for the decadence of Nestorian Christianity—the people had no access to the written record of the Bible, and were therefore without a standard by which to test any new doctrine. They were entirely dependent upon tradition and upon precepts handed down by word of mouth, and therefore more or less unreliable and uncertain.

It was as a result of these various causes that the Nestorian movement declined. All that now remains of it in China and in Central Asia is in the form of certain secret societies, the rules and regulations of which have evidently a Christian origin.

CHAPTER XXIV

THE COMING OF CHRISTIANITY TO CHINA

PART II

IN the thirteenth century the events of history were once more preparing the way for another advance of the Christian faith into Central Asia and China. This time it was the western drive of the Mongol hordes which cleared an open passage enabling Eastern and Western civilizations, for the first time, to make direct contact. Before long Europe became aware that the invading Tatars were not only tolerant of all creeds, but that there were large groups of Nestorian Christians still scattered throughout Asia, and that the Great Khan himself was aware of the Christian religion, and not unfriendly towards it. Gradually the thought of converting the Tatars to Christianity took shape, and friars set out hoping to carry this great purpose into effect. John of Pian de Carpine, a Dominican, was the first of these friars of whom we have any record, and he went as an envoy of Pope Innocent IV to the Court of the Great Khan, near Karakorum. He presented his letters to the monarch, witnessed the enthronement of Kuyuk, and, having done so, returned to Italy.

Meanwhile in 1248 a Tatar embassy arrived at the court of St. Louis of France, in response to which another friar, Andrew of Longjumeau, set forth eastward. Three years later he was followed by William of Rubruck, who, on returning to Europe, left a companion, Bartholomew of Cremona, behind to carry on the instruction of the Tatars. The Khan's request had been for one hundred men competent to teach the Christian religion, but only a very few friars arrived in response to his appeal, and they appear to have been more skilled as diplomats than equipped as missionaries.

The sea-route to Canton was being increasingly used by European travellers, but it was so slow that merchants often spent two years on the journey, the death-roll of passengers was always heavy, and it was much less safe than the overland route. There were now, however, two routes by which travellers from Europe might reach the Far East, but the one considered shortest and safest was still overland.

The pioneer of the Latin Church in China proper was the intrepid John of Monte Corvino, a Franciscan and the first Archbishop of Peking. From two letters written home respectively in 1305 and 1306 we see what progress Latin Christianity had made in the eleven years which he had already spent in Cathay. He addressed himself to the Tatar Dynasty then ruling the land, and though he failed to convince the Great Khan himself, yet Prince George, who was one of the royal clan, from being Nestorian became a Roman Catholic. Monte Corvino himself had built a church in Peking, and reported in a letter which has been preserved that he had bought and baptized one hundred and fifty pagan boys, to whom he taught Greek and Latin and from amongst whom he selected a choir. The influential convert Prince George followed his example and built a second church, twenty days' road journey from Peking.

In 1307 the Pope created Monte Corvino Archbishop of Cambaluc and sent him out six suffragans, all of whom were Italian Franciscans. It would have seemed that the Latin Church was now firmly established in Cathay, but before the end of the fourteenth century Islam had won Central Asia and had closed the trade-route which hitherto had been so safe for travellers, the Tatar dynasty so favourable to Christianity was driven out of China and replaced by the Chinese Ming dynasty, which resumed the exclusive and anti-foreign policy so natural to the Chinese. We hear then of friars fleeing across Asia to the Volga, and then, for nearly two hundred years, there was silence concerning the Christian Church in China.

The revival of Roman Catholic missions dates from 1583, when the Jesuit, Father Ricci, was first allowed to live in Peking, and before his death in 1610 the Jesuit brethren had established missions at Canton, Nanking and Kiansi. Ricci reached China by the sea-route, but it was during his lifetime that the link was completed which established the geographical fact that Peking was actually Cambaluc and accessible to the West both by land and by sea. The renowned missionary traveller Benedict de Goës journeyed from India and across the Gobi towards Peking. He reached Suchow, first town of China within the western fortress of the Great Wall, and there he died, but not before he had despatched a messenger who made contact with the Jesuit Father in Peking. Benedict de Goës was buried by the Moslem people of Suchou in the trackless desert, for they recognized in him a worshipper of the one God, though not a member of the Islamic brotherhood.

A little later Father Verbiest, a learned missionary, was appointed President of the Chinese Faculty of Mathematics by the Emperor Kang-hsi, and before his death about 300,000 Chinese professed conversion to the Roman Church.

* * *

Protestant missionary work in China began, characteristically, when in 1807 Robert Morrison of the London Missionary Society landed in Canton with the immediate objective of translating the Bible into Chinese. Nine years previously the Rev. W. W. Moseley, a British Nonconformist minister, was so profoundly convinced that the peoples of the Far East could never intelligently receive Christianity unless the Bible were translated into their own tongues, that he issued a circular urging the establishment of a society for the express purpose of translating the Scriptures into the languages of the most populous Eastern nations. " Until the Scriptures," he wrote, " are circulated among them the three hundred and thirty millions of China will continue to sit in darkness and in the shadow of death, and to perish for want of knowledge." Later on Mr. Moseley had the unspeakable joy of discovering in the British Museum a manuscript hitherto quite unknown to the public. It was in the Chinese language and was entitled

S. John iii, 16, in Manchurian.   S. John iii, 16, in Mongolian.

དཀོན་མཆོག་གིས་ཉིད་ཀྱི་སྲས་གཅིག་པོ་གནང་བ་ཙམ་དུ་འཇིག་རྟེན་ལ་
བྱམས་པར་མཛད་པས།སུ་ཞང་དེ་ལ་དད་པ་བྱེད་པ་མེད་པར་མི་འགྱུར་གྱི་མཐའ་
མེད་པའི་སྲོག་ཐོབ་པར་བྱའོ།

S. John iii, 16, in Tibetan.

上帝憐愛世人甚至將獨生子賜給他們，叫凡信他的不至滅亡，必得永生。

S. John iii, 16, in Mandarin Chinese.

Quatuor Evangelia Sinice, but proved to be not a direct translation of the four Gospels but a harmony of the Gospels, the Book of the Acts and all the Epistles of St. Paul. It was evidently the work of an early Jesuit missionary.

The discovery of this volume was a great incentive to fresh effort, and in 1804, when the British and Foreign Bible Society was formed, the question of printing it with a view to distribution in China was immediately considered. It was found, however, that the cost of printing and binding one thousand copies would be about two guineas per copy, and the value and accuracy of the translation would need careful consideration. Moreover, there was no agency through which the book could be circulated in China. The discovery of the manuscript, however, had one great benefit —it silenced the opposition of two prominent men—Sir William Jones, author of "Asiatic Researches," and Mr. Charles Grant, a director of the East India Company—both of whom had declared authoritatively that " the Chinese language is not such as to admit of any translation being made into it." A few years later, when Robert Morrison sailed for China, he took with him a copy of this manuscript as his first textbook.

Morrison's letters home reveal some of the almost insuperable difficulties under which he worked. " The Chinese Government is incapable of perceiving the innocence and benevolence of our work . . ." he wrote. " We have to learn in secret and have often had to hide our books and papers. My assistants have again and again run from me through fear. Learning their language is a thing the Chinese do not allow." For three years he toiled with unremitting diligence, and only then felt himself justified in commencing the work of Scripture translation. In 1810 his first book, the Acts of the Apostles, was printed in Chinese from wood blocks. The New Testament was finished in 1814, the Old Testament in 1819, and in 1823 the printing was complete. Morrison's colleague, the Rev. W. Milne, who had joined him in 1813, took up his residence in Malacca, where most of the printing was done, and from where the books were distributed among the Chinese living in Java, Sumatra, Siam, Cochin China and throughout the Malay Archipelago. The expenses were very heavy, and the British and Foreign Bible Society alone spent £10,000 on Morrison's version, but from that hour China had the Bible in the Chinese language.

China seemed prepared in an exceptional way by its national traditions to receive the knowledge of Christianity through the medium of literature. The doctrines of Confucius have been preserved and spread, not by preachers but by means of books; men of letters form the aristocracy and fill all the offices of State, and respect for the printed page is taught throughout the land. Some means, however, had to be devised for distributing the Bibles, and there was as yet no agency through which it could be done; there were no mission stations, no native Christians, and by Imperial Edict the printing or circulation of the Scriptures was punishable by imprisonment or even death. Chinese booksellers in Canton, determined not to forfeit a business proposition, even pasted false titles on the Testaments that they might not be accused of selling Christian books.

For twenty-five years Malacca and Singapore remained the chief centres of distribution, though in 1831-1833 a missionary named Gützlaff made three voyages along the entire coast of China, calling at every port and leaving Bibles with all who would accept them, and in 1835 Messrs. Medhurst and Stevens repeated the experiment. A new epoch for Christian work in China commenced, however, in 1842 when, by the Treaty of Nanking, five ports were opened to trade and the island of Hong Kong was ceded to Great Britain, for in each of these ports missionaries quickly

SUN YAT SEN, FIRST PRESIDENT OF THE CHINESE REPUBLIC

Crown Copyright reserved

GENERALISSIMO AND MADAME CHIANG KAI SHEK EMERGING FROM A
DUG-OUT AT THE " ALL CLEAR "

[Page 144

CHINESE VASE. T'ANG DYNASTY
A.D. 618–906

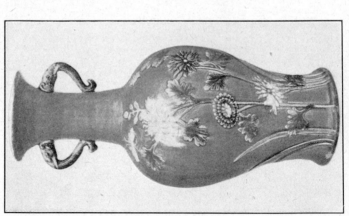

CHINESE VASE. STONEWARE OF
THE XVI CENTURY

BOWL WITH IRON-RED ENAMEL.
XVI CENTURY

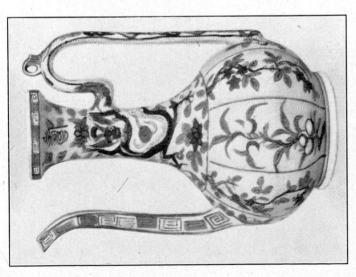

EWER OF PORCELAIN. WAN-LI PERIOD
1573-1619

CHINESE MOSQUE

TEMPLE BUILDING, SHANGHAI

took up their residence and evangelistic work was rapidly developed. As we have seen, the London Missionary Society was first in the field, beginning work in China in 1807. Following this the Dutch Reformed Church entered the field in 1832. The British and Foreign Bible Society appointed its first Agent in 1836.

The American Baptist Society was there in 1843.

The Basel Evangelical Missionary Society in 1846.

The American Board of Commissioners for Foreign Missions, the Church Missionary Society and the Methodist Episcopal Church of America all opened up work in 1847.

The Methodist Missionary Society came in 1851.

The United Presbyterian Church in 1859.

The Danish Missionary Society in 1862.

The Society for the Propagation of the Gospel in 1863.

The China Inland Mission was formed in 1865, with the objective, as its name indicated, of carrying the Evangel into the Inland Provinces. The activities of this Society exercised a great influence upon the thought of other Mission Boards, and demonstrated the possibility of establishing centres far from treaty ports.

The Friends Foreign Missionary Association also began work in 1865.

The Berlin Missionary Society did so in 1872.

The Baptist Missionary Society came in 1877.

From small beginnings missionary effort in China took on very rapid development, and a large number of Protestant Missionary Societies opened up work in China, Manchuria, Mongolia, Sinkiang and on the borders of Tibet.

Sponsored by the British and Foreign Bible Society, translation of the Bible into all the languages and dialects spoken within China and her dependencies has kept pace with the spread of evangelism. All the early versions were issued in the classical style called *Wenli*, which was suited to the fastidious taste of the scholar class, but meant nothing to the unlettered men and women who soon formed the majority of the converts. The literary language is used for all the Chinese classics and has been taught in all the schools, but it is not the speech of any section of the people. It is really a script, not a spoken language. Mandarin is the spoken language of about three-quarters of the whole population of China, the remainder speaking a variety of vernaculars, of which the most important are those of Ningpo, Foochow and Amoy. By degrees books of the Bible appeared in all these various dialects, and in 1919 a revised version of the Mandarin Bible was published under the title Union Mandarin Bible, as each of the principal Missionary Societies had a representative on the Board of Translators. The sale of Scriptures reached its peak in 1929 when the grand total was 13,921,461 copies. These figures represent the joint circulation of the British and Foreign Bible Society, the American Bible Society and the National Bible Society of Scotland.

CHAPTER XXV

THE COMING OF CHRISTIANITY TO CHINA

PART III

MISSIONARY service very soon covered the whole range of Christian activities, and school work established its claim as a matter of primary importance. The Chinese had a national reverence for learning, yet the percentage of illiterates was appalling, and there was a rooted prejudice against the education of girls. The missionary was obliged to begin at the lowest grades of elementary schooling in order to lay the foundation of Western scholar-ship; but each decade witnessed progress which eventually attained full university standard.

In 1876 there were already 289 Mission Schools with 4,909 pupils, and in 1910 there were 3,129 Schools connected with Missionary Societies with an enrolment of 79,823 scholars, besides many Government Institutions modelled on the Western pattern. From the proclamation of the Republic (1912) China's educational programme took vast propor-tions, and at the time of the Japanese invasion she had 42 Universities, 34 independent Colleges, and 32 Technical Schools, in all 108 Institutions of higher learning with a student body of 32,888. It is a magnificent achievement. It was realized from the commencement that women's education would deal a death blow to the iniquitous custom of binding girls' feet, and this strengthened the opposition with which the suggestion of girls' schooling was received. As a matter of fact, as had been anticipated, wherever it became general the foot-binding habit ceased. .

The amazingly rapid growth of literacy in China is one of the most hopeful signs of her determination to remove the handicap under which millions of her people have laboured. Various systems have been introduced in order to teach the masses, and these have resulted in the release of a spate of popular literature which brings books, papers and maga-zines within the reach of all. In Shanghai alone, until its occupation by Japan, more than thirty daily papers were published, and in Free China more than eight hundred dailies still hold their own. Three thousand periodicals are printed in the interior, some of which are *The Modern Critic, The Literary Front, Popular Opinion, Diplomacy, News for the Masses, The Financial Review, New Youth, The Farmer's Weekly, China and the U.S.S.R.*, etc., etc. With the outbreak of hostilities many periodicals ceased publica-tion in coastal towns, so the journalists moved inland to give help as required, and concentrated attention on broadsheets, to be posted on city walls. These presented short articles, poems, and many instructive paragraphs for general reading.

It is evident from the success of all these publications that there is a unique opportunity for Christian Literature Societies to bring the very best books of the West to the Chinese people. " Very few Christian leaders," writes a Chinese, " seem to have yet realized that literature is one of the most important factors for bringing in the Kingdom of God on earth." Christian leaders have expressed surprise to find how little good reading is done by the Christian community, and how little interest is taken by them in that great subject, " What shall the new literates read?" The field has been ploughed and is now ready for the sowers. The vital question is, " Who will get in first?"

Medical missionary effort was for many years handicapped by the distrust and prejudice of reactionary Chinese opinion, but it has finally won the confidence it deserves. The first association of medical missionary doctors was formed in 1887 under the name of *China Medical Missionary Association*. At that time missionary doctors were few, and almost no Chinese doctors had any scientific training; but the number of medical men and women steadily increased, and in 1925 it became the *China Medical Association*, open to all fully qualified doctors, of whom there were now a large number. The C.M.A. holds conferences and provides information on all matters relating to hospitals, but since the outbreak of hostilities its work has been mainly directed to meeting the innumerable demands of emergency conditions.

Among the many Jewish refugees who escaped to Shanghai from Europe were several hundred doctors, and these gladly helped to fill vacant staff appointments on various emergency institutions in Shanghai and in the interior. Thus medical work of a high order is now well established in China, but the credit of arduous and often thankless pioneer work is due to the Christian missionary.

While educational, medical and social services are by-products of the Church's life, the main work of the missionary has been to bring the knowledge of Christ to those who have never heard His name. Slowly but surely a great company of believers has emerged who heard in the Gospel the Word of God to themselves, and responded to His call. Having copies of the Bible in their own language, they have been able to follow intelligently the teaching which has been given to them, and the knowledge of the Scriptures shown by many Chinese Christians would surprise members of the Home Church.

The Church of Christ in China has, in comparatively recent years, undergone periods of severe testing. In 1900, during the Boxer rising, many names from China were added to the Roll of the noble army of martyrs. Then for a period the Church became popular, and its members had to face the more difficult test of remaining true to Christ when all men spoke well of them.

In 1927 there came another difficult period when the spirit of nationalism expressed itself with great vehemence, and an incident when some Chinese students were shot during a demonstration in Shanghai sent a wave of anger through the land. It greatly affected all Church institutions, both educational and medical—in fact any institution controlled by Westerners was temporarily suspect. It was then that the foundations of missionary work were thoroughly tested. Those who had worked under the conviction that all responsibility must finally pass to the Chinese had trained men and women to assume authority, and when the missionaries had to leave there was no insuperable difficulty in carrying on, while those whose point of view was different reaped the harvest of their own short-sighted policies.

The causes of events are always present before their recognition, and for a long time there had been resentment in connection with Church work on the part of those who found themselves under too rigid foreign control. It is now many years since Madame Chiang Kai Shek's father wrote to a friend:

" I have not been to see my parents as yet. Dr. Allen has said I may go during the coming Chinese New Year, and not before then. I am very much displeased with this sort of authority, but I must take it patiently . . . or people at home might think I am a law-breaker, so I have kept as silent as a mouse. When the fullness of time has come I will shake off the assuming authority of the present superintendent. . . . He was the man who wanted to dismiss all the native ministers from preaching a year ago, and he is the man who ignores my privileges and equality. I do not like to work under him. I shall apply for transmission to Japan."

The attitude of the Church in China to the missionary body and its individual members at the present time is best understood by such expressions as the following:

"Missionaries should be selected and sent out in response to the call of the Church overseas for help on specialized lines of service. This includes not only educational, medical and literary tasks, but the important work of training nationals with a view to enriching the evangelistic and pastoral work of the Church and of gradually bearing full responsibility.

" It must be the Church overseas which assigns to the missionaries the work through which their best contribution can be made.

" All missionaries must act as members and servants of the Church overseas, but this would not preclude personal relation to their own Home Church.

" Westerners must act as colleagues to Eastern fellow-workers, and where required serve under their leadership."

It is obvious that such requirements are, from the point of view of many missionaries, most revolutionary, and will greatly alter their relationship towards the body of Christians with whom they are required to co-operate.

In 1922, at a great Missionary Conference held in Shanghai, Chinese leaders expressed their determination that the Church of Christ in China was radically Chinese, and must not be a replica of an English, American or German denominational Church, Chapel or Mission Hall, but truly Chinese. Leadership they had, and the name of Dr. Cheng Ching Yi —a saint and scholar—will always be remembered in relation to the establishment of the National Christian Council of China, which took place in 1922, and has, ever since, served as an affiliating body for Eastern and Western sections of the Christian Church.

One of the organizations most symptomatic of the modern outlook in China is the " New Life Movement." It took form in 1934 under the auspices of the Generalissimo and Madame Chiang, who expressed its purpose in these words: " The New Life Movement calls for the revival of the cardinal virtues of propriety, loyalty, integrity and honour, virtues which have constituted the bulwark of our national existence." The Movement was enthusiastically received, and in pre-war days exercised wide influence through channels of social discipline and service, expressing itself down to the detail of cleaner streets, tidier homes and neatness in dress. With the outbreak of hostilities the leaders saw an opportunity to widen its influence, and since then it has included the training of women for war service, care of war orphans, refugee relief, the development of home industries and of rural and industrial co-operatives, and teaching of the more illiterate members of the community by better educated groups.

The vast bulk of the Chinese nation is still non-Christian, and millions have never even heard the Gospel message, while millions more have decided that the religion of their ancestors is better suited to them than that which they call the " religion of the West." The fact that Red Cross units are at work, that orphanages exist all over the country, that the education of the masses is undertaken by the government, and that the good works of the Christian are praised, though a tribute to humanism, has nothing to do with recognition of Christ as Saviour and Lord. The substitution of a dignified tablet in place of the grotesque idol, or the modern " currency for hell " banknote for the former gold and silver paper at an ancestral sacrifice, does not indicate a change of heart, but merely a change of fashion. Rather must the Christian Church beware lest compromise again confuse the issue and admiration for the expression of Christian love be accepted in place of the radical change of heart required by Christ of His disciples.

At this hour more than any other, every man must have access to the Book which is the only authentic word from God regarding sin, redemption and salvation. For this reason the Bible Societies must be enabled to produce adequate supplies of Scriptures not only in the Mandarin version but also in the phonetic script, the vernaculars of southern provinces, the dialects of aboriginal tribes, and in the tongues of all the nations belonging to China's wide dependencies. The demand is phenomenal, and many new methods of distribution must be explored in order to ensure that the Book and knowledge of its contents become accessible even in the most remote towns and villages, and among the encampments of nomad people. There must also be response from men and women called to these lands and commissioned to preach Christ there by word and by deed. They will be sent as bearers of glad tidings, of good news, and as living witnesses to the power

LAMA PRIESTS AT LAMA TEMPLE, PEKING

MINARET AND MOSQUE BUILT BY TIBETAN-
SPEAKING MOSLEMS

Page 152]

Crown Copyright reserved

CHINESE BOOKSELLER CARRYING HIS STOCK SLUNG FROM BAMBOO
POLES

of the Risen Christ while He is seen to be confirming the word by the results that follow. China and her dependencies, with the many tribes and nations who inhabit them, all wait for a certain answer to the question of every human heart, " Who will show us any good?"

QUESTIONS FOR STUDY-CIRCLES

1. Draw a sketch map of China, inserting boundaries, rivers, mountains, lakes, the Grand Canal, the Great Wall, the Burma Road, and all places mentioned in Chapter XVII.

2. Chinese territory extends from Hong Kong to Siberia and from the Himalayas to the Pacific. Note the outstanding climatic conditions which it covers.

3. Compare the northern and southern Chinese people. What are their chief similarities and differences?

4. China has been extremely backward in developing rapid transport, but very ingenious in devising means of slow transport. Can you suggest some of the causes of this discrepancy and its effect on the people?

5. The Chinese believe that their native products make them completely self-sufficient. Is this so? Consider the matter and form an opinion concerning it.

6. What is your mental picture of a Chinese family, its strength and its weakness?

7. It has been said by a well-known writer that China is the only country in the world where old people feel really happy. Discuss this.

8. Why is Christian literature so important to the spread of Christianity in China?

9. From what you know of the Chinese character, what would you expect to be her great contribution in regard to the Church Universal?

10. Patience is one of the great qualities of the Chinese people. Has this been entirely to their advantage, or have they lost something by it?

11. In a Chinese debating society the assertion was made that China has lost more than she has gained through contact with the western nations (the knowledge of Christianity being excluded). What points could be argued on either side?

12. As a Christian, what would be your approach to a Buddhist (believer in reincarnation), to a Confucian (modelling his life on the conception of a Princely man), to a Moslem (insisting that there is but one God and that the Christian worships two) and to a member of the New Life Movement who maintains that he practises the Christian virtues?

13. The Chinese are remarkable for their tolerance. In what measure does this further their acceptance of Christianity or the reverse?

14. Give the dates of Confucius and name some of his contemporaries in the West.

15. Richard Bell writes: " From one point of view the triumph of Islam in the East . . . may be regarded as the judgment of history upon a degenerated Christianity." If this be correct, trace the chief causes of this degeneracy in Central Asia from the ninth century onwards.

16. What do you know about the Nestorian Monument?

17. What lessons should the modern missionary learn from the rise and fall of Nestorian Christianity in Central Asia?

18. The Empress Dowager believed that it would be fatal for the people of China to slacken their policy of exclusion. The Generalissimo and Madame Chiang welcomed contacts with other nations. Discuss these differing viewpoints and form an opinion as to the wisdom of each.

19. Write a brief and concise account of the so-called

" Boxer Movement " of 1900, and discuss its cause and its effect upon the propagation of Christianity in China.

20. Compare specimens of the Sung, Tang, Ming and Ching periods of art. Note their dates and compare their characteristics.

21. What are the chief differences of outlook in the Old Masters of Western and Eastern art?

22. What do you mean by the expression " Foreign Concession "? Transfer the same principle to London and consider what it would involve.

23. Hong Kong, the Burma Road, the League of Nations, Extra-territoriality. What would you expect the reaction of the average Chinese student to be to each of these words?

24. " Agree to differ but resolve to love." " I am not a member of a foreign Church, I am a member of the Church of Christ in China." " O God, send a revival and begin in me!" Here are three spontaneous utterances by leading Chinese Christians. What had they experienced to call forth such remarks?

25. You have many opportunities of reading missionary books, magazines and circular letters which are also read by English-speaking Chinese. Consider how they would be affected by the reading and analyse their reactions.

26. The missionary is a herald of the Gospel. What personal characteristics are essential to the success of his missionary work?

27. When we speak of the population trekking westward in China what do we mean?

28. Enumerate some of the great changes which must follow as a result of the invasion of China by Japan.

BIBLIOGRAPHY

Author	*Title*
BLAND AND BACKHOUSE	China Under the Empress Dowager
BROOMHALL - - - -	Islam in China
BUCK - - - - - -	Good Earth
	The Young Revolutionary
	Brothers
CURIE - - - - - -	Journey Among Warriors
FOSTER - - - - - -	The Church of the Tang Dynasty
	Then and Now
HAHN - - - - - -	The Soong Sisters
HAN SUYIN - - - -	Destination Chungking
HOSIE - - - - - -	Brave New China
HSIEH CHINGING - -	The Autobiography of a Chinese Girl
JOHNSTON - - - -	Twilight in the Forbidden City
LAUTENSCHLAGER - -	With Chinese Communists
LIN YUTANG - - - -	My Country and My People
	The Importance of Living
	Moment in Peking
PRATT - - - - - -	Great Britain and China
RATTENBURY - - - -	China, My China
ROXBY - - - - - -	China
SMEDLEY - - - - -	Battle Hymn of China
STEWART - - - - -	Nestorian Missionary Enterprise
WALN - - - - - -	The House of Exile

INDEX